T0149533

Nini and Poppie's
Excellent Adventures

Nini and Poppie's
Excellent Adventures

Grandkids, Wine Clubs, and Other ways to

Keep Having Fun

Jerry Zezima

NINI AND POPPIE'S EXCELLENT ADVENTURES
GRANDKIDS, WINE CLUBS, AND OTHER
WAYS TO KEEP HAVING FUN

iUniverse books may be ordered through booksellers or by contacting:

iUniverse
1663 Liberty Drive
Bloomington, IN 47403
www.iuniverse.com
1-800-Authors (1-800-288-4677)

ISBN: 978-1-5320-5662-8 (sc)
ISBN: 978-1-5320-5663-5 (e)

Print information available on the last page.

iUniverse rev. date: 09/11/2018

ALSO BY JERRY ZEZIMA

"Leave It to Boomer: A Look at Life, Love and Parenthood by the Very Model of the Modern Middle-Age Man"

"The Empty Nest Chronicles: How to Have Fun (and Stop Annoying Your Spouse) After the Kids Move Out"

"Grandfather Knows Best: A Geezer's Guide to Life, Immaturity, and Learning How to Change Diapers All Over Again"

PRAISE FOR JERRY ZEZIMA

"I was a fan of Jerry Zezima's hilarious columns in my local newspaper long before I met him. His commentary on daily life, parenting, and, now, grandparenting has always made me laugh."
— *Amy Newmark, publisher, "Chicken Soup for the Soul"*

"Jerry is at it again. Enjoy!"
— *Craig Wilson, former humor columnist at USA Today and author of "It's the Little Things"*

"Jerry Zezima makes every day an excellent adventure. He writes about family foibles with heart and humor."
— *Teri Rizvi, founder and director, Erma Bombeck Writers' Workshop*

"In his three grandchildren, Jerry finally has worthy comedy partners, allowing him to follow in the tradition of great teams of the past such as Moe, Larry, and Curly, Ed Sullivan and Topo Gigio, Key and Peele, and Hillary and Donald. I can't wait until the kids write their own tell-all so Jerry can write the blurb for their book."
— *John Breunig, editorial page editor and columnist, Stamford Advocate*

"Jerry Zezima spins more yarn than a housewife on the prairie, and readers will laugh out loud at some of his tales. They're loaded with puns, humor, and witty observations about this strange world we share."
— *David Trinko, managing editor, The Lima (Ohio) News*

"Jerry Zezima is the king of family humor, Erma Bombeck's male counterpart."
— *Cathy Turney, author of "Laugh Your Way to Real Estate Success" and other books*

"Do you have a warm, 'punny,' and adventurous grandpa? Well, now you do, and author Jerry Zezima finds hilarity everywhere. His antidote to modern stress is an old-fashioned belly laugh and making you feel like family."
— *Suzette Martinez Standring, author of "The Art of Column Writing" and "The Art of Opinion Writing"*

CONTENTS

DEDICATION

For my wife, Sue, and our grandchildren, Chloe, Lilly, and Xavier. Thanks for your unending love, for accepting the sad fact that I am the least mature person in the family, and for making life such an adventure.

ACKNOWLEDGMENTS

To Katie and Lauren, thanks for being such wonderful, loving daughters, smart, accomplished women, and terrific mothers, which means on all counts that you take after Mom, and for putting up with my stupid jokes all these years. Thanks, too, for not minding so much that I am now telling them to your children.

To Dave and Guillaume, thanks for being such great sons-in-law, devoted husbands, and fabulous fathers. Ditto about the jokes.

To John Breunig, editorial page editor and columnist at my hometown paper, the Stamford Advocate in Connecticut, thanks for running my column even though there is ample evidence that it is contributing to the decline of the newspaper industry.

To Johnnie Miller-Cleaves and all the other fine folks at Tribune News Service, thanks for distributing my column to papers nationwide and abroad. See above.

To Mya Barr, Donna Carlson, Rob Espinosa, and the rest of the team at iUniverse, thanks for publishing this book, my fourth for the house. You have once again lowered your otherwise high standards, and I appreciate it.

INTRODUCTION

People often ask if I spoil my grandchildren. "No," I tell them. "That's my wife's job. My job is to corrupt them."

If Sue and I were getting paid for these jobs, we'd be millionaires. But we work for nothing. And nothing could be more rewarding.

That's why there is nothing like being a grandparent, though first you have to be a parent, which should be apparent.

Sue and I love being Nini and Poppie, which is what we are called by our beautiful, precious, smart, sweet, funny, talented, wonderful, delightful, terrific, fabulous (you get the idea) grandchildren, Chloe, Lilly, and Xavier.

We don't see them every day because we haven't won Powerball and still have to go to work, but every day we do see them is an adventure.

We've taken them to the zoo and to the playground. We've gone bowling with them. We've visited the Smithsonian (I'm surprised I wasn't put on exhibit). We've made scrambled eggs, ice cream, and doughnuts. We've sung, danced, and read books. We've changed diapers, something I've done far more for them than I ever did for our own children. We've learned to tell time, ridden on carousels, won prizes at fairs, made friends with cows, blown bubbles, attended preschool graduations, done Three Stooges imitations, made snow angels, splashed in kiddie pools, enjoyed days at the beach, and otherwise had a ball with these kids.

But Sue and I haven't limited our fun to the juvenile set. We've also had a great time with each other. We are, after all, wine club members, which has enabled us to have our own adventures. We go out for pizza, shop at the outlets, do household chores, go to the supermarket, have cocktails on the patio, and generally live life in the slow lane because, at this stage of our lives, who's in a hurry?

We're both in our sixties, which makes us baby boomers who believe that sixty is the new forty. Neither of us is an accountant (Sue's a teacher, I'm a public nuisance), but the math adds up.

This is the perfect time of life because you can still do everything you have always done, but if there is something you don't want to do, you can pull the age card. That means you can finally get out of doing stuff like moving furniture or shoveling snow.

That, you discover, is what your kids are for. It gives you time to do really important stuff — like playing with your grandchildren.

In our case, that would be Chloe, her little sister, Lilly, and their cousin, Xavier.

The cast of characters includes our older daughter, Katie, and her husband, Dave, who are Xavier's mommy and daddy, and our younger daughter, Lauren, and her husband, Guillaume, who are Chloe and Lilly's mommy and daddy.

This book features other characters as well. Some are relatives, some are friends, some are people who have done various kinds of work for us, some are folks I've run into in odd places. I've written about all of them in my syndicated humor column for my hometown paper, the Stamford Advocate in Connecticut.

All of the stories are true. The names have not been changed to protect the innocent. Or, in my case, the guilty

Much of what goes on takes place where Sue and I have lived for the past twenty years, Long Island, New York. But no matter where we have been, we've always had fun, especially in our roles as Nini and Poppie

I hope you have fun, too, while reading this book. Pull up a chair, pour yourself a glass of wine, and join us on our excellent adventures.

1

"Child's Play"

"Spare the Frame, Spoil the Grandpa"

People have said for years that I will end up in the gutter. Little did I know it would happen when I went bowling with my three-year-old granddaughter.

As part of Chloe's birthday celebration, Sue and I went to The All Star in Riverhead, New York, with Lauren and Guillaume for an afternoon of fun and, I will readily admit, humiliation, which is inevitable when (a) you are wearing bowling shoes and (b) you are defeated by a toddler.

I must say in my own defense, pathetic though it may be under the circumstances, that I had not been bowling in years, while Chloe is a regular at the lanes.

Not only that, but she uses a special contraption that is designed to give kids an unfair advantage over incompetent grown-ups such as yours truly. Here's how it works: An adult places a bowling ball on top of this thing. Then a child pushes the ball down a ramp and onto the lane, where it rolls, slowly and steadily, until it knocks over some or all of the pins.

Did I mention gutter guards? They are used so a child's ball can't go where the aforementioned people have long expected to find me.

But none of that mattered because we were there to have a good time, even if, as required in order to use the lane, we would also be keeping score.

After settling in at Lane 20, we entered our names into the overhead electronic scoreboard: Mommy, Nini, Poppie, and, of course, Chloe (who was playing with the assistance of Daddy).

My first ball, I swear to God, went straight into the gutter. I recovered enough to finish the frame with a six.

I didn't feel so bad because Sue's first ball went straight into the gutter, too. In fact, her average roll traveled approximately four inches before the ball plopped into the gutter, although she displayed great versatility by throwing gutter balls on both sides of the lane.

"Bowling isn't my sport," she acknowledged.

But it appears to be Chloe's sport. After Guillaume placed the ball on top of her kiddie ramp, Chloe pushed it onto the lane and typically knocked over most of the pins. By frame five, she had racked up a strike and a couple of spares and was comfortably in the lead when she pushed a button on the control device and wiped out all the information on the scoreboard. The game, essentially, was over.

"I am crediting your granddaughter with the victory," said the nice young man at the counter, likening it to a rain-shortened baseball game. "She beat all of the adults."

Then, sensing my humiliation, he gave us another game for free.

"Try to do better this time," he said with a smile.

I did try. Really. So did Lauren, a streaky bowler, and Sue, who continued to throw gutter balls and even used Chloe's kiddie device and the gutter guards in a couple of frames. They didn't help much.

In one of the later frames, Chloe said, "I bowl with Poppie."

She took my hand as we walked up to the line. Then she helped me throw the ball, which rolled straight down the lane and, incredibly, knocked over all the pins.

"Poppie got a strike!" I exclaimed.

"Poppie strike!" declared Chloe, who must have sensed that I needed assistance, so she gave it to me in the next frame, too. I got a spare.

That helped put me over the top. At the end of the game, my score was 114. Chloe had 99, Lauren 91, and Sue 42.

Chloe, clearly the best bowler in the family, showed a maturity beyond her three years and sacrificed herself so poor Poppie, utterly embarrassed in the first game, could claim victory. In short, she let me win.

I was bowled over. And, thanks to my granddaughter, I didn't end up in the gutter.

"Poppie's French Connection"

Of all the Romance languages, the most beautiful, in my humble opinion, is Pig Latin.

Take this simple phrase: "Hiya, toots!" Translated into Pig Latin, it becomes: "Iya-hay, oots-tay!"

Eloquent, isn't it?

The second most beautiful Romance language is French, in which I am not, unfortunately, conversant. But I am learning it with a certain je ne sais quoi (translation: "Hiya, toots!") with the help of Chloe, who is three.

Chloe is learning French with the help of her daddy, Guillaume, who is from France, a magnificent (magnifique) country that I visited five years ago with my wife (ma femme), Sue (Sue), and some other members of our family (la famille) for the wedding of Guillaume and our younger daughter (fille), Lauren (ditto).

Now their daughter, Chloe, is teaching me (moi) French.

I want to speak it better than I do Spanish, which I took for eight years in high school and college and still can't hold a decent conversation. I know only two phrases: "Cerveza fria, por favor" ("Cold beer, please") and the natural follow-up question, "Donde esta el bano?" ("Where is the bathroom?")

That is why I am sure Chloe will be muy bien (sorry, I mean tres bon) in teaching me French.

According to Lauren, when Chloe went for a doctor's appointment recently, she said to the receptionist, "Je m'appelle Chloe," which means "My name is Chloe."

"Did she just speak French?" the stunned receptionist asked.

"Yes," Lauren replied, though she should have said, "Oui."

The next time I saw Chloe, I said, "Je m'appelle Poppie."

She smiled, no doubt at my pathetic pronunciation, and said, "Poppie!"

I was babysitting her and thought it was a good time for a French lesson.

"Bonjour, Chloe," I said.

"Bonjour, Poppie," she responded.

That was pretty much all I knew. But I was about to get a crash course. Chloe loves books and always wants me to read to her, so I was not surprised when she handed me a book starring her favorite character, Peppa Pig. The title: "Une Journee Avec Peppa" ("A Day With Peppa").

Yes, it was in French.

If you read Chloe a book in English and stumble over a word, she will make you repeat it.

"My God (Mon Dieu)," I thought, "this is going to be terrible (terrible)."

I began to read: "Ce matin, Peppa se reveille."

I had no idea what I just said, but it didn't matter because Chloe didn't correct me. I thought, however, that the word "reveille" meant Peppa was in the Army, though the drawing on the page showed that she was in her bed at home and was waking up at seven o'clock in the morning.

It was obvious from subsequent drawings that the little pink porker was getting ready for school.

I trudged on: "Et prendre le petit-dejeuner tous ensemble, c'est encore mieux. Parole de Peppa!"

Chloe smiled and turned the page, a clear indication that my reading was d'accord (OK).

When Peppa got to school with her classmates, there was this line about the teacher: "Madame Gazelle, leur maitresse, est fantastique!"

Then Peppa went home for lunch: "C'est pizza et salade au menu!"

Afterward, she went to the park with her friends: "L'apres-midi, Peppa retrouve ses amis au parc."

At dinner, Peppa's father, Daddy Pig (Papa Pig), made his famous soup (fameuse soupe), after which Peppa had to brush her teeth ("apres avoir mange, il faut toujours se laver dents") and go to bed ("bonne nuit!").

Through the entire reading, Chloe didn't stop me once, so I felt confident enough to add, "The end," which I didn't know in French (la fin).

But that was all right because Chloe paid me the ultimate compliment: "Merci, Poppie!"

I had passed my first French (francais) test. One of these days, with Chloe's help, I will speak it fluently.

Then, of course, I will teach her Pig Latin.

"Big Girl Weekend"

The surest sign that a toddler is getting big is when she becomes more mature than her grandfather.

Two other signs are when she gets her own bed and has her first haircut.

Both of those things happened to Chloe in what was dubbed, in case you missed the celebration, Big Girl Weekend.

Since she was born three years ago, Chloe had slept in a crib, which prevented her, as some grandfathers have been known to do, from getting up on the wrong side of the bed.

I don't know what the wrong side of the bed is, unless it is against a wall, in which case you will hit your head when you get up and promptly fall back to sleep. Since I am off the wall, I have never had this problem. That's why I have always thought that the right side of the bed is the top.

Anyway, Chloe had begun trying to climb out of her crib, a sure sign that it was time to get her a bed.

When Chloe heard the news from Lauren and Guillaume, she was very excited. Sue chimed in, saying Chloe was going to get a "big-girl bed," which made her even more excited.

When I added my two cents, which Chloe put in her piggy bank, she said, "Chloe's a big girl. And Poppie's a big boy."

"Poppie has a big-boy bed," I said, hoping I wouldn't wake up on the wrong side of it and slam headfirst into a wall.

Lauren and Guillaume shopped around for a twin bed and a box spring, but naturally there were complications because one store offered one deal and another store offered another and never the twin did meet.

One day, Guillaume and I, thinking outside the box spring, lugged a box containing a bed, not a spring, back to one of the stores. Later, I went home and fell fast asleep in my own bed.

But rest assured, it all turned out OK because, on a recent Friday, Chloe's new big-girl bed was delivered. She took to it like a fish to water, even though it's not a water bed, and went right to sleep that night, probably dreaming of her first haircut, which she got the next day.

On Saturday morning, Sue and I went over to see the bed, which is higher than ours and a lot more comfortable. It also has two mattress guards, presumably so Chloe can't get up on the wrong side.

"Do you like your bed?" I asked Chloe.

"Yes, Poppie!" she chirped. "I'm not a baby. I'm a big girl."

And she proved it even further when Lauren, Guillaume, Sue, and I took her to Hairport Salon in Port Jefferson, New York, for her first official haircut.

"She looks like Shirley Temple," said Valerie, a very nice stylist who had the important assignment — and, if I do say so, the honor — of trimming and shaping Chloe's blond curls.

Chloe sat calmly in a chair, holding three purple brushes while Valerie snipped her underlying baby hair. Chloe even helped by handing Valerie one of the brushes.

When the haircut was over, everyone told Chloe she looked beautiful.

Chloe smiled and bit into a cake pop that Lauren had given to her for being so good.

It was a fitting end to Big Girl Weekend. The next celebration will be this Saturday, on Big Boy Weekend, when Poppie gets up on the right side of the bed and goes for a haircut. I may even have a cake pop.

"Poppie Goes to School"

When I was three years old, I knew my ABCs. Unfortunately, I didn't learn the rest of the alphabet until I was in high school.

Even now, Chloe is way ahead of me. So I was thrilled when I was asked to assume actual adult responsibilities and, for the first time, bring Chloe to school.

Because Lauren and Guillaume had an early morning appointment and would be gone before Chloe got up, I had to sleep over and get her ready for what promised to be an exciting day.

To facilitate matters, Lauren gave me a list of instructions. The first, written in her very neat cursive, was: "Wake up."

This is extremely important, unless you are deceased, in which case the sleepover becomes permanent.

Instruction No. 2: "Change pull-up."

"I don't wear pull-ups. At least not yet," I informed Lauren, who rolled her eyes (I rolled them back) and said, "Chloe does. Take her to the potty. I'll leave her outfit in her bedroom. Bring it downstairs and get her dressed after breakfast."

I perused the remaining instructions, which included what to give Chloe for breakfast (three-quarters of a cup of milk, microwaved for thirty seconds; one strawberry yogurt; and one slice of multigrain toast).

"I spoke with Mrs. Kramer," said Lauren, referring to Chloe's preschool teacher, "and told her you were dropping off Chloe and that you would pick her up after school. I gave her a description of you, but you may have to show her your driver's license."

I felt like an escaped felon, but I guess you can't be too careful these days.

The next morning, I followed Instruction No. 1 to the letter and woke up.

"Do you know what to do?" Lauren asked as she put on her coat.

"Yes," I replied confidently. "I have to go to the potty and then have breakfast."

Lauren rolled her eyes again and said, "And don't tell Mrs. Kramer any of your stupid jokes. She might call the cops."

About fifteen minutes after Lauren and Guillaume left, Chloe woke up. I went upstairs to her bedroom and opened the door.

"Poppie!" she exclaimed.

"Good morning, Honey!" I chirped.

I followed the remaining instructions (potty, check; pull-up, check; breakfast, check; outfit and hair bow, check; brown shoes, check; hat and coat, check; backpack and sippy cup, check; carseat, check) and drove Chloe to school.

I waited at the door with her as a bunch of other kids and their mothers showed up. The young women smiled at me, but I could tell what they were thinking: "Who the hell is this geezer?"

A few minutes later, Mrs. Kramer opened the door.

"Hi, Mrs. Kramer," I said, introducing myself. "I'm Poppie."

"Hi, Poppie," said Mrs. Kramer, who greeted Chloe by saying, "Good morning, Chloe!"

"Good morning, Mrs. Kramer!" said Chloe.

"Do you need to see my driver's license?" I asked Mrs. Kramer.

"No," she responded pleasantly. "Lauren gave me a description of you. I'll see you later."

"Bye, Chloe," I said.

"Bye, Poppie!" said Chloe, who went inside with her little friends.

I smiled at the mommies and drove back to Lauren and Guillaume's house, where I made myself useless for a couple of hours before returning to pick up Chloe.

As the door opened and the children exited, Mrs. Kramer held up a bag and said, "Here you go, grandpa!"

I thought she was talking to me, but she was referring to Mike, a fellow grandfather who was picking up his grandson, Mason.

"We're the only grandpas here," I said.

"I know," said Mike. "But I've done this before. Mrs. Kramer knows me."

"No one would mistake us for mommies," I said.

Mike nodded and said goodbye. I took Chloe's hand and said goodbye to Mrs. Kramer, who smiled and said, "You did a good job."

"Did I pass the test?" I asked.

"Yes," said Mrs. Kramer. "You can tell Chloe that Poppie got a gold star."

"Do the Ride Thing"

As a geezer who has learned that life has its ups and downs, as well as its twists and turns, especially with small children who aren't prone to motion sickness, I have often been taken for a ride.

That's what happened when I took Chloe to the Mattituck Strawberry Festival on Long Island and accompanied her on all the best kiddie rides.

This brought back fond if unnerving memories of the many times I took Katie and Lauren on roller coasters, Ferris wheels, and other vertiginous vehicles designed to scramble brains, overturn stomachs, and test the bladder retention of adults whose young companions were required to complete the physical and psychological damage by screaming directly into your ears and causing a lifetime of auditory damage before the white-knuckle experience was mercifully over.

As it turned out, I loved these rides even more than my daughters did.

We were regular (and sometimes irregular) visitors at the St. Leo's Fair and the Annunciation Greek Festival, both in our hometown of Stamford, Connecticut; Quassy Amusement Park in Middlebury, Connecticut; Lake Compounce Family Theme Park in Bristol,

Connecticut; Playland in Rye, New York; Six Flags Great Adventure in Jackson, New Jersey; and Busch Gardens in Williamsburg, Virginia.

We never visited Disney World in Orlando, Florida, possibly because I didn't want to get in line while the girls were in kindergarten and finally reach a ride after they would have graduated from high school.

Also, I wasn't keen on the idea of having to take out a bank loan just to buy a day pass and then melting to death in the blazing heat.

That's why the Strawberry Festival was so much fun: It was low-key and inexpensive.

As soon as I arrived with Chloe and Guillaume, we scoped out the rides, some of which were tame and meant for younger kids like Chloe, and some of which were wild and meant for older kids like me.

I went on the tame ones with Chloe anyway.

We couldn't find the Teacups (maybe because it wasn't four o'clock), so we went to the carousel, where Chloe shunned the horses (she won't grow up to be an Olympic equestrian, I guess) and instead rode the bench (which I used to do in Little League).

First, Guillaume went with Chloe, then I did.

"Are you having fun, Sweetheart?" I asked as we went around and around and waved to Guillaume every time we passed by.

"Yes, Poppie," Chloe answered, though I could tell she wanted to go on something a bit more exciting.

She's too young (and short) to go on crazy rides like the Octopus and the Giant Swings, so we settled for the Wiggle Wurm, which not only proved, as every fisherman knows, that worms can't spell, but was so cramped for adult riders that, as my knees rammed into my nostrils and my boxer shorts rode up into an area generally reserved for medical specialists, I could have been the lead singer for the Vienna Boys Choir.

It bounced and jounced along, swooping up, down, and around at a speed that seemed excessive under the constrictive circumstances but probably wasn't much greater than that of a car driven by a little old man creeping in the left lane with his turn signal on.

Finally, we went on the Fun Slide, which required Chloe and me to climb a set of stairs not appreciably shorter than those in the Empire State Building and then, settling onto a canvas bag, whoosh down at a speed that could have broken all existing records at the Bonneville Salt Flats.

It was so much fun that we went three times.

Next year, Chloe will be old enough to go on some of the bigger rides. My heart, stomach, and boxer shorts can't wait.

"The Grandfather Playground Society"

To steal a line from Groucho Marx, who is dead and can't sue me, I would never belong to any club that would have me as a member.

But I made an exception on a weekday afternoon when I was indicted (sorry, I mean inducted) into a prestigious, exclusive, and, I can proudly say, entirely dubious organization called the Grandfather Playground Society.

The founding members were yours truly and two guys named Jeff and Steve. I was there with Chloe, who is three; Jeff had Madison, two; and Steve had Aliya, also two.

The first thing Jeff said to me was: "I am going to have a heart attack."

That's because he had already been chasing Madison around for an hour.

"I think I'll join you," I responded, because I had just raced with Chloe from slides to swings and back again and was feeling a bit short of breath.

Unfortunately, Chloe doesn't yet know CPR, which stands for Collapsed Poppie Resuscitation.

Steve, meanwhile, was following Aliya on a tricycle (she was riding it and he was walking in circles behind her because there wasn't enough room on the seat for both of them) and was grateful he was getting a breather.

"This beats running," he noted.

"When you have grandchildren," I said, "you don't have to join a health club."

"It saves a lot of money," Jeff said.

"And you can use the savings to buy beer," I pointed out.

"I could go for one right now," Steve chimed in.

Then all three of us went back to the slides with our granddaughters, who wanted us to accompany them. This required us to put the kids on our laps and swoosh down at breakneck speed, absorbing jolts to our tailbones before coming to a screeching halt on the hard plastic surface about two feet from the end, the result being that we were almost catapulted skyward with toddlers who thought it was fun but didn't realize that their grandfathers nearly suffered grievous injuries that could have transformed us into falsettos.

"Let's go again, Poppie!" Chloe exclaimed. Her new friends agreed.

"What do you do for joint trouble?" Jeff asked after the third trip.

"Move to a new joint," I answered.

Instead, we moved back to the swings, where Madison, Aliya, and Chloe were secured in their seats while Jeff, Steve, and I pushed them and officially convened the meeting.

"Being a grandfather is the best thing in the world," I said.

"Yes," agreed Steve. "And after you're done playing with your grandkids, you can give them back."

"Speaking of backs," Jeff said with a wince, "mine is sore as hell."

"But it's worth all the aches and pains," I said. "In fact, it makes you young again."

And I proved it, after the girls were done on the swings, by chasing Chloe up and down a nearby hill, then going to another set of slides, where I didn't have to accompany her but did have to catch her at the bottom and run back around to watch her as she climbed the steps.

Meanwhile, Jeff and Steve were running after their granddaughters, who don't move as fast as Chloe because they are a year younger but who nonetheless can take the wind out of any geezers who happen to be their grandfathers.

A little later, we met up again at the park entrance.

"It's time for a nap," Steve said as he looked down at his tired granddaughter.

"You look like you could use one, too," Jeff said.

"We all could," I added with a yawn.

On that note, the first meeting of the Grandfather Playground Society ended. The three of us, granddaughters in tow, limped back to our cars and wished each other happy healing.

"The next time we get together," I suggested, "let's go to a spa. If it's good enough for their grandmothers, it's good enough for us."

"It's Chloe Time"

I live in a different time zone than everybody else — right now it is 8:49 a.m. Eastern time, 5:49 on the West Coast, and 12:27 on Mars — so I was a little late in finding out that Chloe got a watch.

I have had one watch in my life. It was given to me as a college graduation gift by my parents, who liked to remind me that I was born more than three weeks past my due date and hadn't been on time for anything since. The watch was one of those digital numbers that didn't have two hands, which required me to use two hands to tell the time. It was a pain in the wrist.

Not long after Sue and I were married, our apartment was burglarized. Her watch was stolen. Mine was left behind. It wasn't even good enough for thieves.

At the time (4:32 p.m.), I resolved never to wear a watch again. And I haven't. I am in a deadline business, but I don't care what time it is. If I need to know, I'll look at the clock on the wall. If I don't see a wall, I know I'm outside and that it's time (midnight) to come in.

Now Chloe, who was born a week early, has a watch. It was given to her by her parents, though not as a college graduation gift because even kids these days don't grow up that fast.

At least it's not digital. It has a purple band with pink and white flowers and a face with two hands, which means Chloe doesn't need two hands to tell the time.

What she does need is somebody to teach her how.

That, against all odds, is where I come in.

Whenever Chloe visits, she wants me to read her favorite literary masterpiece, "Tick and Tock's Clock Book." Subtitled "Tell the Time With the Tiger Twins!," it's the compelling if somewhat repetitive tale of two feline brothers who are baffled by time, which makes them no better than me. Of course, I never tell that to Chloe. Instead, I begin reading:

"Brrringg! The alarm clock rang so loudly it made Tick and Tock jump out of bed.

" 'What time is it?!' said Tock.

"Tick went to look at the clock.

" 'Um … the big hand … Not sure,' he said. What time did the clock say?"

"What time did the clock say, Poppie?" Chloe asked during a particularly dramatic reading.

"It didn't say anything," I replied. "Clocks can't talk."

Chloe giggled and said, "Silly Poppie!"

According to the drawing on the page, it was 8 a.m., even though it was 3:15 p.m. in my house, so I helped Chloe move the plastic hands — the big one to the twelve, the little one to the eight — on the clock in the upper right corner of the book.

The rest of the story follows the messy Tiger Twins through their day, during which they can't figure out what time they are supposed to leave for school (8:30), finish their painting project (10:15), have lunch (12:30), go home (3:30), and have dinner (4:45).

But the best is saved for last. That's when Tick and Tock's mother, who has just cleaned up one of their many messes, announces, "There, it's all tidy now. Look, it's 8 o'clock, time for bed."

But the clock on the wall says otherwise.

"Tick and Tock looked at the clock and said, 'No, it's not! It's 7 o'clock. We have another hour to play, hooray!' "

In one of the greatest endings in all of literature, the Tiger Twins' mother can't tell the time.

"Maybe," I said to Chloe as I closed the book, "Tick and Tock should buy her a watch."

"You Must Have Been a Beautiful Baby"

Ever since my second grandchild, Lilly, was born last month, people have been asking who she looks like.

It's hard to say because babies change by the hour, and need to be changed just as often, but I can tell you this: Because Lilly is so beautiful, she doesn't look like me.

Figuring out who babies look like is one of the great mysteries of modern science. People — especially parents and grandparents, but also aunts, uncles, cousins, friends, neighbors, and complete strangers who happen to be passing by and can't help but comment on how cute the kid is — see who and what they want to see when they see a baby.

If you ask me (you didn't, but I am going to answer anyway), Lilly looks like her mother, Lauren, who is my younger daughter and is, no thanks to me, beautiful.

When Lilly's beautiful sister, Chloe, was born three and a half years ago, people (see above) said she looked like her father, Guillaume, a handsome guy with a full head of dark hair, which Chloe had, too. Now, however, Chloe looks just like Lauren, right down to the blond curls.

When Lauren was born, everyone said she looked like me. When her older sister, Katie, was born, everyone said she looked like my wife, Sue. Now people say Lauren looks like Sue and Katie looks like me. I can believe the former, because Sue is beautiful, but not the latter, because Katie is beautiful and I, while not exactly Freddy Krueger, am not exactly Brad Pitt, either.

But back to babies, who are living (and crying, eating, sleeping, and pooping) proof that beauty is in the eye of the beholder. It has been my observation that they look like whichever side of the family is seeing them at any given moment.

These family members will always comment on how beautiful the baby is and will then add that the little darling has all the traits of either the mother or the father, depending on which one is a direct relative.

It becomes more complicated (and pretty weird) when the comments involve body parts. For example, someone might say, "She has your nose."

No one ever said that about Katie and Lauren, thank God, because if one of them had my nose, she wouldn't have been able to lift her head until she was in kindergarten.

Eyes are also big. Mine are. They're bloodshot, too. Still, they are the feature that people most often ascribe to the mother, the father, or, in some cases, the passer-by who turns out not to be a complete stranger.

"She has my eyes," relatives love to say.

The truth is that if the kid has your eyes, you couldn't see, which is likely to be the case because, the vast majority of the time, nobody else agrees.

Even if you're right, you'll soon be wrong. The baby's eyes, nose, ears, mouth, hair, hands, or feet, which you could swear are just like yours, will soon resemble someone else's. Then that person will say, "She looks just like me!"

What is indisputable is that all babies, whether they are children or grandchildren, are beautiful. OK, so maybe some of them aren't, but they're not related to any of us. And if they are, they have my nose.

So go ahead and see yourself in the new addition to your family. Brag that the little girl or boy is the spitting (and sometimes regurgitating) image of you when you were a baby, or looks like you now, or has all the traits that make everyone in your family so good-looking.

Like a broken clock, you'll occasionally be right.

But know this: My granddaughters, Chloe and Lilly, are the most beautiful children on earth. If anyone disagrees, it will, of course, get ugly.

2

"Grape Expectations"

"Stomping With the Stars"

$\mathbf{I}$f I ever get my own sitcom, which I am actually working on, I'd call it either "Everybody Loves Jerry" (Ray Romano can star) or "I Love Jerry" (Lucille Ball can't star because Lucy's in the sky with Desi).

In the pilot episode, I would re-create Lucy and Ethel's famous grape stomping routine. It would be based on real life because I went to Riverhead, New York, for a Grape Stomp Party at Martha Clara Vineyards, where I am a member of the wine club.

I do not pretend to be an oenophile with a discriminating palate, mainly because my files are disorganized and I don't like to paint, but I prefer red wine because it is, according to my doctor, over-the-counter heart medicine. And for a geezer like me, that's very important.

So when I received an email invitation to the Grape Stomp Party from Gina Messa, Martha Clara's bubbly hospitality manager and empress of fun, I readily accepted. Then I had a glass of merlot, just to set the mood.

Merlot grapes, as it turned out, were one of two kinds that attendees would be stomping, the other being riesling, a white variety that Sue prefers. Unfortunately, she couldn't make it to the party, so I chose merlot and hoped the grapes I stomped with my bare feet wouldn't make their way into a bottle of Martha Clara Merlot Jerry, the sniffing of which would certainly be something to sneeze at.

"No," Gina assured me as the party got underway, "we wouldn't do that to our customers. In fact, the grapes you stomp will be thrown out."

That must have come as a relief to the other one hundred and thirty attendees, who ate a light lunch in the vineyard's converted barn before going out back for the stomping.

There, all in a row, sat eight bins, each of which could hold a quarter-ton of grapes but contained only half of that to give attendees room to stomp them.

"The world of wine can be pretentious and snobby," said Juan Micieli-Martinez, Martha Clara's winemaker and general manager, "but this is going to be fun."

No one had more fun than Juan's five-year-old son, Benecio, who had already stomped both red and white grapes.

"They're squishy!" he told me.

"He can't drink wine yet," said his mother, Bridget, who used to work in the industry, "but he can help make it."

When it was my turn, Gina asked me to take off my flip-flops. She looked at my naked tootsies and said, "You should have worn nail polish."

"Since I'll be stomping merlot grapes," I replied, "I'll get a red-icure."

"You're really getting into the spirit," said Gina, who then helped me get into the bin, where we immediately started dancing in a shin-deep mass of merlot makings.

A crowd of attendees, wineglasses in hand, cheered us on as Gina twirled me around so dizzily that it felt like I'd already had a couple of glasses of wine.

After a few minutes, she helped me out of the bin and hosed off my feet, which were covered in juice and had crushed grapes between the toes. Benecio was right: They were squishy. His father was right, too: It was a lot of fun.

"A couple of years ago," Gina said, handing me a towel, "two women showed up dressed as Lucy and Ethel."

"If I don't get my own sitcom," I told her, "we could have a dance show, 'Stomping With the Stars.' "

"I bet we'd win," Gina said. "And we could celebrate with wine." She smiled and added, "I know a guy who makes a mean merlot."

"This Caveman Is a Cool Guy"

People who know me and are willing to admit it (which narrows the field considerably) will gladly tell you that I have frequent bouts of brain freeze and that everything I say should be taken with a million grains of salt.

Aside from margaritas, which I like because they're cold and salty, and have been known to reduce my brain cells to practically zero, never has this sensational combination been more welcome than when I spent time in a salt cave and later was flash-frozen in a cryotherapy chamber.

The place to enjoy these invigorating experiences (not including margaritas) is Port Jeff Salt Cave in Port Jefferson, New York. Billed as "an integrative wellness center," it's owned by the husband-and-wife team of Rich and Marcy Guzman, both of whom are nurses who know that laughter is the best medicine.

As Marcy told me before I sat in a group session in the cave, "Salt doesn't cure anything but ham."

"I'm a ham," I replied.

"Then you'll be cured," she said.

Inhaling salt air can decrease inflammation (good news for my big head), detox the blood (I'm not type O, but I do occasionally have a typo), and send nutrients to my organs (too bad I don't play the piano).

I joined seven other people, ranging in age from twelve to eighty-four, in the salt cave, which looks just like — you guessed it — a hockey arena.

No, actually, it looks like a cave. It also looks like a beach because it contains ten beach chairs, arranged in a circle, but instead of sand, the floor is covered with salt crystals. The room is dimly lit with twinkling ceiling lights that resemble the night sky. There also are vents that release salt air and a sound system that pipes in a soothing recording by Marcy.

At the beginning of the forty-five-minute session, which costs forty-five dollars per person, Marcy said the salt air would open our sinuses.

"My sinuses are already open until nine p.m. on Thursdays," I said.

The other customers shifted nervously in their beach chairs.

But everyone relaxed when Marcy closed the door and started the recording, which took us vicariously on a nature walk, over the river and through the woods, where we bypassed Grandmother's house and encountered several creatures that evidently had escaped from either a zoo or "The Jungle Book" but proved to be good omens that led us back to where we started, safe, sound, and satisfied.

"How do you feel?" Marcy asked afterward.

"Salty," I responded. "And peppery. It was wonderful. I have an inner warmth."

I had an outer cold when I went back a week later for my own version of the movie "Frozen."

I was greeted by Rich, who asked me to strip to my skivvies and don a pair of socks and gloves before entering the small, cylindrical chamber, where the temperature would drop to two hundred and sixty-five degrees below zero.

"I'll end up being like a Mrs. Paul's fish stick," I said.

"Don't worry," Rich replied. "Your wife can thaw you out in the microwave."

He added that during the three-minute session, which costs forty dollars, I'd be enveloped by a nitrogen vapor that would, among other benefits, help my body release endorphins, kill fat cells, and block pain.

"The first minute is refreshing," Rich told me as I stood in the one-person chamber with my hands at my side and my head peering over the closed door. "The second minute is invigorating. And the third minute is 'talk me through this.' Ready?"

I gulped and nodded. Rich turned on the machine. Vapor started to rise and caress my skin, invading my pores and turning my body into what seemed like a block of dry ice. I felt, as Rich promised, refreshed and invigorated.

"Talk me through this," I said as he counted down the last minute.

"No need," he said. "You're doing great."

When it was over, I stepped out of the chamber, the coolest guy on earth.

"Between the two sessions," I told Rich and Marcy after I got dressed, "I feel like a new man."

"The salt air and the cold air really help," Marcy noted.

"The only thing cryotherapy couldn't help is my brain," I said. "It's already frozen."

"The Brew Crew"

As a home brewer who once brewed beer in my own home without, miraculously, blowing the place up, I have great admiration for practitioners of the craft of creating craft products that go down smoothly without coming back up the same way.

That's why I quenched my thirst for knowledge by taking a brewing tutorial with Paul Komsic, brewmaster at BrickHouse Brewery and Restaurant in Patchogue, New York.

Paul, thirty-two, started at BrickHouse as a customer and now, seven years later, is brewing the popular establishment's many fine products, including the one we would be making, a nacho IPA that Paul planned to call Nacho Mama.

This gave me hope, as a BrickHouse customer myself, that I would eventually become the brewmaster, though it might take me twice as long because I am twice as old as Paul.

"How was the beer you brewed at home?" Paul asked.

"Surprisingly good," I told him. "I called it Jerry's Nasty Ale. I don't know why, but it had a smoky taste. My wife and some neighbors tried it and nobody had to be hospitalized."

"That's always a good sign," Paul commented.

"After that, I retired from brewing," I said. "But I'm coming out of retirement today."

Joining me in this class, which I hoped to graduate magna cum lager, were three guys who are home brewers and have no intention of retiring: Chris Cordano, fifty-seven, a tennis instructor, and the Homeyer brothers, Gregg, fifty-nine, an engineer, and Glenn, fifty-two, an electrician.

Offering his able assistance was assistant brewer Brian Smith, twenty-three, who, Paul said, "is me when I was that age."

"Who were you?" I wondered.

"I was still me," Paul answered, "but I wasn't making beer. I was drinking it. Now I do both."

The first thing we learned in the class, which started at eight a.m., was that beer makes a fine breakfast treat. BrickHouse had kindly supplied bagels and coffee, but we got to sample small amounts of the brewery's latest products as the tutorial went along.

The first order of business was learning the steps involved in making beer. Actually, there were three steps that led up to a platform, on either side of which was a mash tun and a kettle. Both are huge. The mash tun, for example, holds eleven hundred pounds of grain.

I got to find out when Paul asked me to dump in some of the thirty pounds of raw tortilla chips that were our brew's key ingredient. Chris, Gregg, and Glenn each got a turn as well.

Also important were Saaz hop pellets, which Paul said would, if you ate one, "set your mouth on fire."

So I ate one. It set my mouth on fire. Fortunately, I had a glass of beer, which quickly doused the flames.

In went the rest of the pellets, along with other ingredients such as yeast, which Paul said eats the sugar that has been converted from grain to create alcohol.

Along the way, we learned that brewing goes back to the Middle Ages, when the process involved running beer through fish bladders.

"Now I know where the expression 'drink like a fish' comes from," I said. "And we're in our middle ages, so we're carrying on a great tradition."

We also got to glimpse the inside of the mash tun as Paul was cleaning out the grains that would be sent to feed cows at a nearby farm as part of the "Brew to Moo" program.

"Does the milk come out with a head on it?" I wondered.

"No, you can't get beer from a cow," Paul said as he removed the screen at the base of the tun, which is, on a much smaller scale, what my classmates do when they make beer at home.

"I have a false bottom," Gregg said.

"How do you sit down?" I asked him.

The tutorial, which was fascinating and lots of fun, took about four hours, after which Gregg, Glenn, Chris, and I had lunch: delicious burgers and, of course, beer, though not the nacho IPA, which wouldn't be ready for another two weeks.

"I can't wait to taste it," I told Paul. "And when you retire, let me know. If BrickHouse needs another brewmaster, I'll be available."

"Portrait of the Artist As a Wine Man"

As a painter specializing in bathrooms, bedrooms, and cats, who used to get splattered when I was painting the first two, I will never be mistaken for van Gogh (when I go for a haircut, I still get both ears lowered) or Picasso (my wife would kill me if I painted a nude model instead of the hallway). I can't even draw a good salary.

But I exchanged walls and fur for a canvas of glass when I took a Paint & Sip class at Martha Clara Vineyards.

It was the first time I had ever painted wineglasses, but I was assured by the very nice and very talented instructor, Maggie Carine, that my artwork would be worth toasting.

"It may not end up in the Louvre," said Maggie, twenty-two, a steward at Martha Clara and a graduate of Pratt Institute in Brooklyn, New York, "but it will hang proudly on your wine rack at home."

Each attendee in the thirty-person class, which cost thirty-five dollars for wine club members such as yours truly, was treated to a glass of either Solstice Blanc or, my preference, Syrah, because red wine is not only good for the heart but, as Maggie noted, "good for the art."

She also gave me several kisses (of the Hershey's variety) to add to the palate, if not the palette.

As I took my seat at one of the tables, I noticed that everybody was given two wineglasses to paint.

"If you mess up," Maggie told the class, "you have an extra chance."

Also in front of each attendee was a clear plastic plate with dollops of red, pink, purple, and white paint, as well as two paintbrushes, one small for delicate work, the other large in case I got carried away and, fueled by wine, painted the entire vineyard.

In addition, we each had two sets of stencils with the shapes of lips, hearts, and the letters XO, all of which signified love. We also were given foam-tipped stampers so we could festoon our glasses with polka dots.

"Tape the stencils to the inside of your glasses and trace around them on the outside," Maggie instructed us. "Then color in the shapes. Be creative!"

That was all I needed to hear. Like van Gogh, I painted a self-portrait on my first glass. Using my stamper, I dotted two white eyeballs. I dabbed my small brush in red paint and made the eyes bloodshot. For the finishing touch, I painted a pair of purple pupils, which isn't easy to say when you've been drinking wine.

Then I stamped a big red nose under the eyes. Under the nose I drew a purple mustache. Under that, I traced white lips. I topped it all off with purple eyebrows.

"That's genius!" exclaimed Dianne Sykes, who sat at my table with her sister, Cat, and their mother, Suzanne, all of whom got into the spirit of things with creative paintings of their own.

Cat, for example, wrote "Girls rule, boys drool" on one of her glasses.

"How much wine have we had?" she asked, to which Dianne and Suzanne answered in unison: "Not enough!"

Maggie also was impressed with my artistic creation.

"Awesome!" she declared.

Thus inspired, I finished my first glass with a red heart, a pink XO, and a series of multicolored polka dots. I used my stamper and small brush to create a dotted and striped base.

On my second glass, I flipped the letters and drew a pink, red, white, and purple OX. "I'm as dumb as one," I explained to the ladies, who politely disagreed. I also drew a red heart with an arrow through it, stamped some dots, painted the base red with my big brush, and, with my small brush, put the finishing touch near the top of the glass by autographing it with a red "Jerry."

"You did great," Maggie told me when the class was over.

"Thank you," I replied modestly. "As Picasso might have said, I'll drink to that."

"Color Me Beautiful"

This little piggy went to market, this little piggy stayed home, this little piggy had roast beef, this little piggy had none. But my little piggies, instead of crying wee wee wee all the way home, said the hell with it and went for a pedicure.

Sue, who gets pedicures all the time and whose feet are beautiful, thinks mine aren't. So, to convince her that a little pampering wouldn't be like putting lipstick on a pig, I arranged to be beautiful, too, by having shiny red nail polish put on my piggies.

I put my best foot forward, followed by the other one, when my office was visited by Marianella Aguirre and Jennifer Yepez of Green Spa on the Go, a mobile spa and nail studio in Forest Hills, New York.

Employees could get manicures or pedicures. Even though this is a digital age, and my digits sometimes have hangnails, I decided not to put the man in manicure and instead wanted a trained professional to cure the two titanic tootsies that make me a biped.

That unenviable task fell to Jennifer, who is twenty-eight and has been working at the spa for a year.

"I like your socks," she said, pointing to hosiery embroidered with fish.

"I'm not wearing socks," I replied. "The doctor says this rash should clear up in a couple of weeks."

Jennifer looked stunned.

"I hope you don't think my feet smell like fish," I told her.

"No," she said with a smile of relief as I removed my socks.

"Still," I noted, "you should have worn a gas mask."

"Your feet aren't so bad," said Marianella, thirty-nine, who owns Green Spa on the Go.

"My wife thinks I have the ugliest feet on earth," I said.

"Don't worry," Marianella responded. "Jennifer will make them beautiful."

And she did. It took a lot of work, but Jennifer's expert technique rubbed me the right way.

"Be careful," I warned. "I'm ticklish."

"OK," she said, giggling along with me as she massaged my right foot, which she anointed with cream and oil after clipping my toenails and using a pusher to clean them.

"They're too cuticle for words," I declared.

They were doubly so after Jennifer performed the same wonderful routine on my left foot (not starring Daniel Day-Lewis).

As Jennifer worked her magic, Marianella told me that Green Spa on the Go has clients throughout the metropolitan area, including my hometown of Stamford, and that some of her most notable customers have been former New York Knicks stars Kurt Thomas and J.R. Smith.

"Those guys are huge," Marianella said. "Their feet are really challenging."

"Bigger than mine?" I asked, adding that they are size eleven.

"Yours are baby feet," she assured me.

And, baby, did they feel good. Now all I needed was nail polish.

"Men are going with bright colors these days," Marianella said. "How about red?"

"Why not?" I replied, choosing the shiniest shade, which Jennifer expertly applied to my nails.

"They glow!" I chirped, paying Marianella a bargain price of twenty dollars and giving a nice tip to Jennifer, who in turn gave me a pair of banana yellow, open-toed pedicure slippers, which I had to wear until the polish dried.

When my colleagues saw my glossy hoofs, they could barely contain their excitement.

"Wow!" Kevin gushed.

"I love your toes!" Francesca enthused.

"You have nice feet for a guy!" Janelle exclaimed.

The person I really wanted to impress was Sue. When my shift was over, I put my socks and shoes back on and drove home, where I told her about my pedicure.

"Don't tell me you got nail polish, too," she said.

"Yes," I replied. "Red."

"Oh, my God," she said. "Let me see."

I took off my shoes and socks. Sue looked down.

"What can I say?" she did say. "They're lovely."

"Too bad it's not summer," I said. "Then the whole world would see that I no longer have the ugliest feet on earth."

"Que Syrah Syrah"

When it comes to wine, I have a discriminating palate, so I know that whites go with lighter foods, such as Twinkies and Mrs. Paul's frozen fish sticks, and that reds pair well with meatier offerings, like hot dogs and Slim Jims.

But even I, a person whose prodigious proboscis has sniffed so much wine that I often need a decongestant, had a lot to learn when I met Jeff Saelens, a true oenophile who taught a Wine 101 class at Martha Clara Vineyards.

Accompanying me was Sue, who is something of a wine connoisseur herself (she prefers a glass of chardonnay, out of a box, with one ice cube). The only other students were Brittany Rosen and Chase Smith, a very nice young couple who not only were delightful to talk and drink with, but who guaranteed that, unlike in high school or college, I would graduate no lower than fourth in my class.

Jeff, seventy-eight, a wise and witty wine wizard (say that five times fast after you've had a snootful of sauvignon), isn't snooty or snotty even though he is sophisticated. He also is a retired business development expert who used to own a wine shop in Saratoga Springs, New York, and has a degree in neurochemistry from Harvard Medical School.

"Can I call you doctor?" I asked him as the class began.

"I've been called worse," Jeff replied with a wry smile.

Then he handed out the course materials, including a map of France, which Sue and I visited in 2011 for Lauren's wedding. In preparation for the trip, I learned such important French words as "bonjour," "bon appetit," and, of course, "Bon Jovi."

The map was divided into France's premier wine regions, such as Loire Valley and Rhone Valley but not Silicon Valley, where California grapes, not to mention Apples, are grown.

In front of each student were two wineglasses, into which Jeff poured Tang instant breakfast drink.

No, actually, he poured wine, starting with reds, which I prefer, and finishing with whites, which Sue likes.

"First, we will try pinot noir and Syrah," Jeff said as he gave us a small amount of each.

"The Syrah is drier and the pinot is sweeter," Sue remarked, to which Brittany and Chase agreed.

Showing my impressive expertise, I noted, "They're both better than Boone's Farm."

Jeff said the grapes for both wines grow better in "a cold, miserable climate," adding that the best Syrah is from Rhone Valley and the best noir is from Burgundy.

"Syrah dates back two thousand years," Jeff said. "Pinot noir is even older: three thousand years. Bordeaux, on the other hand, is only two hundred to three hundred years old. Still," Jeff added dryly, "that's even older than I am."

Our education continued as Jeff talked about different kinds of grapes, as illustrated in our materials, as well as various types of soil, including the sandy loam of Long Island, where the maritime climate also contributes to what we all agreed is the excellence of Martha Clara's wines.

Having sipped our way through the reds, which made my eyes the same color, we went to the whites, which I really liked even though I don't normally drink them.

Jeff also discussed food pairings, the fermentation process, and wine consumption by countries (France and Italy consume the most while the United States is near the bottom).

"Don't blame me," I told Jeff. "I'm doing my best to make America grape again."

Jeff thanked me for my patriotic efforts and finished by saying that we all passed Wine 101 with flying colors.

"The colors are red and white, right?" I asked.

"Don't make me revoke your diploma," Jeff said.

Brittany, Chase, Sue, and I didn't get sheepskins, or even grape skins, but we did get a well-rounded education from a man I would nominate as teacher of the year.

"You're a good student," Jeff told me.

"Thank you," I replied. "In Wine 101, I'm tops in my glass."

3

"Creature Features"

"How to Bathe a Dog"

Over many years of living in a household where the fur frequently flies, I have learned that the best way to get rid of fleas, ticks, and other pests, and to stop incessant scratching, is to bathe the itchy sufferer with a liberal application of special soap, rinse thoroughly, and follow up with a treat.

It works on dogs, too.

Sue, whose grooming is impeccable, suggested that our granddog, Maggie, be given a bath. Maggie doesn't have fleas, ticks, or other pests. In fact, she is impeccably groomed herself. But she does have dry skin that causes her to do what people often tell me to do: go scratch.

So Sue thought it was time for a bath.

"Can't I just take a shower?" I asked.

Sue sighed and said, "Hook up the hose outside and get the doggy shampoo."

It's a good thing we weren't doing this in the bathroom because Maggie doesn't like to be bathed. She's totally unlike our late pooch, Lizzie, who loved being given the spa treatment

She'd just stand there, soaking it all in. After she was dried off and brushed, she'd go back inside and preen. Then she'd plop down and take a nap.

That is the difference between dogs and humans: After a bath or a shower, a person has to go to work to keep man's best friend in the style to which he or she has become accustomed.

And we call dogs dumb animals.

To bathe a dog, you will need the aforementioned hose and shampoo, as well as a towel. That's for the dog.

For you, there's a much bigger list: three pairs of rubber gloves, a bathing suit (or, if it's chilly, a raincoat), flip-flops (or galoshes), goggles, a shower cap, fishing waders, or, depending on how much the dog shakes, rattles, rolls, and otherwise dislikes the bath, scuba gear.

You'll also need a collar and a leash. So will the dog.

Step 1: Put the collar on the dog, attach the leash, and, with one hand, hold firmly. With your other hand, hold the hose. With your third hand, turn on the water. If you have an assistant, he can turn on the water. I was assisting Sue, so that was my job. Since dogs have four hands, you wonder why they just can't bathe themselves.

Step 2: Wet the dog, being careful that the dog, in its excitement, doesn't wet you. Then hold on to the leash for dear life because most dogs won't like this and will pull you with such force that one arm will end up being six inches longer than the other one. If you have a mastiff, you may also be dragged for three blocks. It will hurt like hell if fences are involved.

Step 3: If the previous step goes well, apply the shampoo or soap and rub it into the dog's coat. At this point, your fingers will pop through your first set of rubber gloves. Put on another pair and continue washing. Be sure to get behind the ears, around the haunches, and along the tail. If you have a bulldog or a schnauzer, or if you are washing yourself, this last part will be unnecessary.

Step 4: Don your last pair of rubber gloves and rinse the dog off. Then stand back or the dog will shake enough water on you to fill an Olympic-size swimming pool. At this point, fur will be all over your legs, feet, and face, in your hair, and wedged permanently under your fingernails.

Step 5: Dry off the dog with a bath towel.

Step 6: Burn the towel.

Step 7: Brush the dog to get off the rest of the loose fur. You will notice that the dog has dandruff. Ignore it and give the dog a treat.

Step 8: Give yourself a treat. A beer will do.

Step 9: Have another beer.

Step 10: Take a shower. Just like your dog did, you'll need one.

"Joking Till the Cows Come Home"

Even though I have always been more apt to milk a joke than a cow, which can create udder confusion (see what I mean?), I have long wanted to be a gentleman farmer.

First, of course, I'd have to become a gentleman, which would ruin my reputation, or what's left of it.

Then I'd have to buy the farm, which both my banker and my doctor say I am not ready to do.

So I did the next best thing: I went to Ty Llwyd Farm in Northville, New York, on the North Fork of Long Island, and met Dave Wines, who is both a gentleman and a farmer.

I also met June-Bug, a calf who has developed a bond with Chloe.

Chloe previously visited Ty Llwyd, a Welsh name pronounced Tee Luid, meaning "Brown House," with Lauren, a member of the Southold Mothers' Club, which arranged the trip.

"The kids had a nice time," Dave recalled. "June-Bug took a liking to your granddaughter. She gave her lots of kisses and wanted to follow her out."

"Maybe June-Bug will like me, too," I said hopefully.

But first I watched as Dave meticulously planted a row of carrots. It was in a part of the thirty-acre farm on the east side of the, yes, brown house. At the entrance, where there's a west side story, visitors are greeted with these signs: "New York Permitted Raw Milk," "Chicken Manure," and "Caution: Ducks."

Dave, who's sixty-seven and fit as a fiddle, even though he doesn't play one, was on his hands and knees, holding a little plastic doohickey (a farming term meaning "doohickey") that contained carrot seeds. He used his right index finger to tap the seeds, one by one, into a long indentation in the dirt.

"Do you like our modern equipment?" asked Dave, adding that the farm has been in his family since 1872.

As he inched his way along, a process that took half an hour, Dave told me about an uncle of his who lived off the land and was, as a result, strong and healthy.

"He was in his eighties and his doctor had put him on a special diet," Dave remembered. "He came over one day and said he wasn't on the diet anymore. I asked him why. He said, 'My doctor died.' "

Dave isn't on a special diet, even though his doctor is still alive, but he does abstain from alcohol.

"When people find out what my last name is, they say I should open a winery," Dave said. "But there are enough of those out here. Besides, I'm a teetotaler. I drink milk."

I have more than made up for Dave's lack of wine consumption, but I am now sold on his milk, which is the best I have ever tasted.

His son Christopher, who lives on the farm, is Ty Llwyd's "milk man," said Dave, adding that he has another son, Thomas, who lives in Boston, and a daughter, Judy, who lives in upstate New York.

"They're in their thirties," Dave said. "I forget their exact ages because the numbers keep changing. It's hard to keep up."

Dave's wife, Liz, was born in Wales, where she and Dave were married.

"Today is our forty-second anniversary," Dave announced proudly.

When I wished the delightful couple a happy anniversary, Liz said, "I'm celebrating by collecting eggs."

She said the farm's twelve hundred chickens produce sixty-five dozen eggs a day. She also said Ty Llwyd has thirty-three cows.

"How much milk do they produce?" I asked Dave.

"A lot," he answered, adding, "I told you I'm bad with numbers."

After giving me a tour of the farm, which has plenty of modern equipment, Dave introduced me to June-Bug, who was in a fenced-in area with her fellow calves: Cassandra, Cricket, Flower, Millie, and Twinkle. They all had name tags on their ears.

"Hi, June-Bug," I said. "I'm Chloe's grandfather."

The sweet calf walked up and started kissing me with her large, rough tongue. The others kept their distance.

"She likes you," Dave noted.

"It must run in the family," I bragged.

"When she's old enough, you should come back and milk her," Dave said. "And that's no joke."

"Lions and Tigers and Beers, Oh, MY!"

In the immortal words of Dr. Doonothing, otherwise known as yours truly, if I could talk to the animals, what a neat achievement that would be. But would a tiger or a camel, bird, reptile, or mammal, really, truly want to talk to me?

That's what I hoped to find out, without being eaten in the process, during trip to the Bronx Zoo, where I trekked with Sue and Lauren, as well as Chloe and Lilly, both of whom were first-time visitors who soon learned that some of the most fascinating creatures walked on two legs and talked to the animals with a New York accent.

We heard them chatter (most of what they said was either incomprehensible or unrepeatable) during a stampede into the zoo, which was overrun with humans because it was Wednesday, when admission is free and the animals get to see what wildlife is really like.

The first denizens we saw were bison, which were once almost hunted to extinction, prompting Lauren to remark, "They make really good burgers."

Then we flew into the World of Birds, which housed, among other fine feathered friends, a guira cuckoo.

"Who's a cuckoo?" I asked Chloe, who looked up at me and chirped, "Poppie!"

The next exhibit was Tiger Mountain, featuring a massive Amur (or Siberian) member of the species that earned its stripes when Chloe commented, "Just like Tick and Tock, the Tiger Twins," referring to the feline siblings who star in a book that teaches kids how to tell time.

By then it was time for lunch (not, thank God, for the tiger, which looked directly at me and licked its chops), so we found a shady spot and gobbled up turkey sandwiches. I didn't feel guilty because turkeys are among the few animals that don't reside at the zoo. It wouldn't have been the case with bison burgers.

As we were finishing, a visitor started yelling at one of her kids (not the goat variety), who ran off faster than a cheetah, further incensing the woman, who brayed, "My house is more of a zoo than this place!"

The scene drove me to drink, so I went to the watering hole and ordered three beers for the adults in our group.

"May I please see an ID?" Tiffany D. asked me.

"God bless you!" I gushed. "I haven't been carded in decades."

"You're looking young in those sunglasses and that hat," she said with a wink and a smile. "In fact," added Tiffany, who couldn't have been more than thirty, "you're looking younger and younger all the time."

"I'm going to come back," I said after I paid her (and left a nice tip).

"OK!" said Tiffany. "Come back and I'll card you again."

As we strolled off, a woman pushing a stroller stopped so her young daughter could say hello to Chloe and Lilly, each of whom was in a stroller, too.

"That's a good idea," the merry mom said when she saw our refreshments.

"You're going to get a beer?" I asked.

"Of course," she answered. "Why do you think I come to the zoo?"

Another woman passed by with her kids in tow and said, "I wish someone would push me around in a stroller."

Sue, who worked up a sweat pushing Chloe, said, "It's a good thing I go to the gym."

A good thing, indeed, because there was plenty more to see, including a polar bear, two grizzly bears, several giraffes, a herd of zebras, and a caravan of camels, which Chloe liked because, as she noted while the beasts of burden masticated disgustingly, "It looks like they're chewing gum."

The only creatures smart enough not to come out were the lions, which disappointed everyone because they were, naturally, the mane attraction. But we did hear them roar from wherever they were hiding, which I hoped wasn't behind my car, where we headed after a long but exciting day.

If I weren't driving, I would have gone back for another beer so Tiffany D. could card me again. At the zoo, it's called animal magnetism.

"The paper Chase"

As an old newspaperman living in a digital age, I am often asked if print will survive. My answer is yes, and for a very important reason: You can't wrap fish in a website. Besides, what are you supposed to do, housebreak your dog on an iPad?

That's why my columns, aside from their obvious benefit of being a cure for insomnia, are so valuable.

If one thing has irrevocably changed, however, it's newspaper delivery, which used to be done by kids on bikes. Now it's done by adults in cars.

In my never-ending quest for column material that can be used by puppy owners to keep their carpets clean, I rode with Lucille Marshak, a newspaper carrier whose best delivery on a dark and stormy night wasn't the newspaper but, fittingly, a dog.

I met Lucille at a gas station at 3:45 a.m. and climbed into the back of her 2011 Kia Sedona, which already has nearly two hundred thousand miles on it and was filled with hundreds of newspapers that Lucille unfailingly delivers, every day except Christmas, through rain, snow, sleet, and gloom of night.

On this gloomy night, it was rain that Lucille had to drive through.

I told her that Lauren used to deliver the Stamford Advocate when she was about twelve and that I once took over for her on a Sunday morning when she was sleeping at a friend's house.

"It was murder," I added. "I had to lug those heavy papers in a bag around the neighborhood. And I didn't even have a bike."

"Kids don't do that anymore," said Lucille, who is sixty-one and for the past twenty-five years has been delivering Newsday of Long Island, where I now live.

As we made our way through the wooded back roads of Lucille's long and winding route, which was eerily illuminated by the headlights of her car, a dog suddenly appeared out of the fog.

"I spoke with the owners earlier," said Lucille, who began at one a.m., "and promised I'd be on the lookout for the dog."

The dog apparently was on the lookout for Lucille, who pulled over and, at my suggestion, opened the back door. The pooch, a beautiful husky, hopped in and shook herself off, giving me the shower I didn't have time to take.

"Do you have to go to the bathroom?" I asked the dog. "We have plenty of newspapers."

The grateful canine, who didn't take advantage of my offer, for which I was grateful, slobbered me in kisses.

When Lucille pulled up to the dog's house, her sibling owners, Chris and Jenna Dooley, both in their twenties, came running out. Their father, Charles, stood at the door.

"I was walking on the wet road in a pair of socks, calling her in the rain," said Chris, adding that the dog's name is Dakota and that she's almost two years old. "My friend was over and when he opened the door to leave, she scooted out."

It was now 4:15, way past Dakota's bedtime.

"Come on, Dakota, let's go inside," said Chris. But Dakota didn't want to leave, preferring to snuggle with me. Eventually she relented and went with Chris, who put her on a leash. "Thank you so much," he said.

"Aren't you forgetting something?" asked Lucille, who extended her hand out the driver's-side window and said, "Here's your paper."

For the next four hours, Lucille regaled me with stories, like the one about the woman who came out to get the paper naked, and the one about the angry guy who chased her in his car and tried to run her off the road because he didn't want an advertising supplement.

She also showed me how to make a perfect hook shot, left-handed (she's a righty) and over the roof of the car, to get the paper to land in subscribers' driveways.

Then there was the Stolen Paper Caper, which occurred on the route of Lucille's husband, Ron, who co-owns the family delivery service, which has included their three now-grown children.

"Two women were arrested for taking papers because they wanted the coupons," Lucille recalled. "Ron and I were interviewed on TV."

Ironically, a guy in my neighborhood has been stealing papers, including mine, while he walks his dog.

"Maybe the dog isn't housebroken," suggested Lucille, who has two dogs of her own and plenty of canine friends on her route.

"If it will help," I said at the end of a fascinating night in which I saw how hard Lucille, Ron, and other newspaper carriers work, "I'll give the guy copies of my column. His dog will be greatly relieved."

"Junkyard Dog Tags"

According to Zezima family legend, which goes all the way back to last week, Sue is so proficient at chopping down trees, bushes, and other massive flora that she is known far and wide as Paula Bunyan.

I, her faithful companion, am known even farther and wider as Jerry the Dumb Ox.

It was in this capacity, which otherwise is about a six-pack, that I was charged with hauling a mess that I was afraid included Audrey II, the giant plant in "Little Shop of Horrors," to the dump, where I met Teddy the Junkyard Dog.

This shocking example of horticultural horror began when Sue went on a chopping spree and took down several humongous growths whose stems, trunks, and branches were roughly equal to those of a California redwood. And she did it not with a chainsaw but a hand saw, which is easier than using a seesaw.

When I saw, I said, "Who's going to cart all this stuff away?"

Sue pointed the saw at me.

I refrained from making a cutting remark and dutifully dragged the whole thing to the curb in the hope that the Town of Brookhaven, New York, where I live, would take it away.

There it sat for three weeks until I got a letter that was headlined: "Notice before summons." It went on to say I was in violation of a town ordinance by having litter described as "loose oversized branches" on my property. It also said I would be subject to "a potential fine and a possible misdemeanor charge" if I didn't take care of it.

I called the Department of Waste Management and spoke with a very nice woman named Maureen.

"Look," I explained, "I'm a geezer with a bad back and a history of kidney stones. I'm doing my best. Have mercy."

Maureen was sympathetic and said, "I got one of those notices before I started working here." Then she added, "You have to cut up the branches and either put them in containers or bundle them. It's probably easier just to load them into your car and bring them to the landfill. If you're a town resident, there's no charge."

Consoling myself with the thought that the worst things in life are free, I stuffed everything into the back of my SUV, which stands for Sequoia Utility Vehicle, and drove to the landfill.

That's where I met Teddy, whom Jim Croce would not have described as "meaner than a junkyard dog."

"He's more like a teddy bear, which is how he got his name," said his owner, Nancy Blomberg, adding: "It's a very exciting day. This is Teddy's first trip to the dump."

Teddy, a terrier mix who was born in Puerto Rico, seemed to take it in stride.

"He's a rescue," Nancy said. "He's six or seven years old, I'm not sure and he's not telling, but I've had him for a year and a half."

Teddy, who was sitting in Nancy's lap on the passenger side of a 2003 Chevy pickup truck, gave me a high paw through the open window.

"Woof!" I replied.

Just then, Nancy's friend Micky McLean, who had been hauling stuff out of the back of the truck, came around and introduced herself, saying she is a former Marine.

When I told her I'm a newspaper columnist, Micky said, "I thought so when I saw you interviewing the dog. What's the matter, the Marines wouldn't take you?"

"The Marines have standards," I said. "They're looking for a few good men, and obviously I'm not one of them."

Micky, who served honorably from 1977 to 1986 and is now retired, asked if I needed help unloading the branches from the back of my car. When I gratefully accepted her kind offer, she got her trusty cultivator, which is a three-pronged rake, and in the span of about seven seconds cleaned out my trunk.

"Next time, cut down the trees and bushes yourself instead of making your wife do it," Micky commanded.

I saluted and said, "Yes, ma'am!"

At that, Teddy barked.

"He's a dog," Micky said. "He knows something about trees and bushes, too."

"Fat Cat on a Thin Roof"

It has been said, probably by Andrew Lloyd Webber, that a cat has nine lives. If that's true, it means the cats in our humble home had thirty-six.

It also means I should win a Tony Award because my version of "Cats" ran even longer than Lloyd Webber's, twenty-seven years to his eighteen and 9,855 daily performances to his measly 7,485.

Unfortunately, the show ended recently when Bernice, the last of our four flaky, friendly, and frequently flummoxed felines, went to that big litter box in the sky.

Sue and I got our first cat in 1989, when we bowed to the pressure of Katie and Lauren, who were then nine and seven years old, respectively, and adopted Ramona, a little black and white cutie named for Ramona Quimby, the star of the Beverly Cleary children's books.

Ramona's claim to fame was that she made it into "Who's Who of Animals," even though, as it said in her entry, "An intelligence test pitting Ramona and a loaf of Wonder Bread proved inconclusive."

Ramona went from aloof to affectionate in 1995, when we adopted a dog named Lizzie, who was so sweet and lovable that Ramona must have figured, if indeed she was capable of rational thought, that if she didn't shape up, she would stop getting all the attention and lose her crown as the family princess.

That did not stop her, however, from eating the boiled chicken that was part of Lizzie's diet. Lizzie, in turn, ate Ramona's cat food.

In 1998, when we moved from Stamford to Long Island, I started getting strange calls at work.

"Meow," purred the voice on the other end of the phone.

"Who is this?" I asked the first time it happened.

It was Lauren, who said she wanted a cat.

"You already have a cat," I told her.

"I want a real cat," Lauren insisted. "Ramona's an idiot."

Enter Kitty, another black and white cutie whose personality was the polar opposite of Ramona's. She was Miss Congeniality and, at a year old, proved it by getting pregnant.

One of Kitty's kitties was Bernice; another was Henry, the only other male in the house besides me, but since he was a mama's boy who loved Sue and Lizzie exclusively, it didn't even count.

Ramona, who turned out to be sweet and even smart in her own way, despite not getting along with the other three cats, lived to be almost twenty. Henry, who was never the same after Lizzie passed away, was stricken with a sudden illness a year later and died at twelve. Kitty died at seventeen.

That left Bernice, who was perhaps the quirkiest of them all.

While her mommy, Kitty, was a little bit of a thing, Bernice was the feline equivalent of the Goodyear Blimp. And she hated to be picked up, which was just as well because anyone who tried would have either gotten a hernia or been scratched to death.

This did not explain how Bernice, who was not appreciably smarter than Ramona, hoisted herself onto the roof of our two-story house. Practically every day, Sue and I would discover that Bernice was stuck up there and was meowing at a bedroom window.

We theorized that she climbed a nearby tree and dropped with a thud onto the roof, though we are still not sure how she did it considering the tree was a fair distance from the house and Bernice weighed about as much as a full-grown male orangutan.

The tree was old and starting to rot, so we had it taken down before both it and Bernice crashed through the roof. Perhaps not coincidentally, her climbing adventures abruptly ended.

But her quirkiness didn't. She loved to be petted and would jump onto Sue or me while we were watching TV, purring contentedly during shows that were appropriately mindless.

Now she's gone, the last of our four family felines, and it's the end of an era. Like Ramona, Kitty, and Henry before her, Bernice was the cat's meow.

4

"Food For Thought"

"The Breakfast Club"

Because I am so culinarily challenged that both the fire department and the nearest emergency room have to be on alert whenever I try to get creative in the kitchen, I will never be a short-order cook.

But Chloe has all the ingredients to be one: She's short, she follows orders, and, as it turns out, she can cook.

I discovered this when Chloe stayed overnight with me and Sue, who's pretty hot in the kitchen. She does all the cooking in our house with the exception of Saturday morning breakfast, which I make for myself because Sue, perhaps wisely, thinks it's safer to have just a muffin and a cup of coffee.

I prefer to have a lot to eat because breakfast is one of my three favorite meals of the day. So I fire up the stove and make eggs and sausage.

On this particular morning, Chloe was there to lend a little helping hand.

First, we got up, which is always recommended if you want to have breakfast or, generally, a long life. On weekends, I like to sleep in (which is better than sleeping out, especially if it's raining) and get up in time to have a late breakfast. The best thing about having a late breakfast is that as soon as you're done, it's time for lunch.

Chloe, on the other hand, likes to get up with the chickens, whose eggs we would be using to make an early breakfast.

We chose two eggs, a white one and a brown one.

"The brown one has a nice tan," I told Chloe.

"A nice tan!" she repeated.

Then she got her little step stool, which she ordinarily uses to wash her hands after going potty, and brought it into the kitchen. She stepped up so she could reach the counter and, carefully following my instructions, which I often don't follow too carefully myself, cracked the white egg. It started to run, so I helped her dump the contents, including a few small pieces of shell, into a glass bowl.

"Be careful or the yolk will be on you," I said.

Chloe didn't get Poppie's lame joke, but she giggled anyway.

She did the same when I said, "Don't shoot until you see the whites of my eggs."

Sue, who was within earshot, rolled the whites of her eyes.

We repeated the process (minus the jokes) with the brown egg.

Next I asked Chloe to place three sausage links in a pan. Only two came out of the box.

"Where's the other one?" I asked Chloe. "It must be the missing link."

At this, Sue exited the kitchen.

Chloe fished the third link out of the box and placed it in the pan, which I put on the stove. I turned on the heat.

"Be careful, Honey," I said. "It's hot."

"It's hot, Poppie!" Chloe declared as she turned her attention back to the eggs, which she whipped into a creamy mixture with a whisk. She did a much better job than I usually do.

Then I got another pan, into which Chloe poured the eggs. I put the pan on the stove, next to the one with the sausage, and returned to the counter to slice a bagel before putting it in the toaster.

"Do you know what kind of bagel this is?" I asked Chloe. When she was stumped, I said, "Poppie seed!"

"Poppie seed!" she echoed with a big smile.

After Chloe used a wooden spoon to stir the eggs in the pan to a perfect consistency, I placed them, along with the sausage and the toasted bagel, on a plate. Then we went over to the kitchen table, where she sat on my lap to share a delicious breakfast.

I wouldn't be surprised if Chloe got her own cooking show. Until then, I can proudly say that making eggs with her is a delightfully mad scramble.

"On a Cart and a Prayer"

If it weren't for Sue, I would have starved to death long ago. Not only is she a great cook (her specialties include everything, which is exactly what I like), but she does all the food shopping. Only illness can prevent her from the swift completion of her appointed eye of rounds.

So when she got sick recently, I had to go to the supermarket. By myself. For the first time in almost thirty-nine years.

"Here," Sue said between sneezes, handing me a shopping list. "You don't have to get too much. Do you think you can handle it?"

"Of course," I said confidently. "I'll just put the cart before the horse's aft."

"If you come back with everything," Sue said wearily, "it will be a miracle."

When I arrived at the store, I met Ken Fehling and Richard Cunnius, who also were shopping for their wives.

"My wife doesn't shop," said Ken, who retired as a college director of residential operations. "So she sends me."

"Do you go back home with everything on the list?" I asked.

"Always," Ken said. "My wife thinks I do a good job."

"I don't think mine does," said Richard, a retired electrical engineer. "When I get back home, she'll say, 'Did you get it on sale? Did you do this? Did you do that?' Then she'll discover that I forgot something. I guess I'm not a good shopper. But if my wife can't go, she sends me."

We stood in the produce section, getting in the way of other shoppers, all of them women who seemed annoyed that three geezers were blocking their way to the lettuce, and talked about wives, kids, and grandchildren before I said, "I have to go to the deli counter to pick up some cold cuts. Nice meeting you guys."

"You, too," said Richard. "Good luck."

"Check off every item on your list," Ken suggested. "That way, you won't forget anything."

When I got to the deli counter, it was so crowded I couldn't get to the machine to take a number.

"I'll get it for you," said Maddy Spierer, an artist who owns a design company. She handed me number fifty-seven. The guy at the counter yelled out, "Number forty-five!"

"I guess we'll have to wait," I said.

"You looked lost," Maddy noted.

"It's my first time shopping alone," I said.

"You'll be OK," Maddy assured me. Then she realized she had taken two tickets, numbers fifty-four and fifty-five, so she handed me the latter. "It'll speed things up," said Maddy, a mother, a grandmother, and a veteran food shopper. When her number was called, she said to me, "You're next!"

"I'm not going to get bologna because I'm already full of it," I told Maddy. But I did pay it forward by giving my number fifty-seven to a woman named Tanya, who had number sixty-two. When I told her my wife had sent me shopping, Tanya smiled and said, "Smart woman."

A few minutes later, in the canned food aisle, I saw a tall gentleman with a black suit and a clerical collar.

"Are you a priest?" I asked.

"I'm a Methodist minister," the Rev. Amos Sherald responded with a warm smile.

"You're just the man I'm looking for," I told him. "This is my first time food shopping by myself. My wife said that if I came back with everything on the list, it would be a miracle."

"Did you remember to bring the list?" Rev. Sherald asked.

"Yes," I replied.

"It's a miracle!" he said.

And, lo, I felt the hand of God guiding me through the rest of the store, making sure I did, indeed, get everything Sue wanted me to buy.

When I arrived home, I told her about my supermarket adventure and especially about my encounter with Rev. Sherald.

Doubting Sue would not believe until she had checked the bags. "He was right!" she exclaimed. Then she added, "How would you like to go food shopping for me next week?"

"I don't think so," I said. "After all, miracles don't happen every day."

"Trouble's On the Menu"

When I was sixteen, I got my first job. I was, improbably, a waiter at the now-defunct Parkway Deli in Stamford.

In pretty short order, even though I wasn't pretty or even a short-order cook, I was fired for what I must admit were two very good reasons: I ate the place out of knishes every day for lunch and, in case you are wondering why the deli went under, I was incompetent.

After a hiatus of more than four decades, I got back into the service industry by working as a waiter at the Modern Snack Bar in Aquebogue, New York.

I came up with the potentially disastrous idea after Sue and I had dinner at the popular family-style restaurant and were waited on by Anilee Bishop, who deserves a medal, or at least a raise, for being my mentor when I returned a couple of weeks later to see if I could drive yet another eatery into the ground.

I arrived at the worst possible time — a busy Saturday night — with Sue, Lauren, Guillaume, and Chloe.

"Are you ready to go to work?" asked Anilee, who seated us in the large rear dining room.

"Yes," I said confidently, promising that I would spare the place the humiliation of having me on staff by waiting my own table.

"If anybody in your family is as tough a customer as you are, you're going to be in trouble," said Anilee, adding that she was fired from her first waitressing job for spilling water all over the silk dress of a rich lady in the Hamptons. "It was my first day," she recalled. "And my last."

But Anilee, thirty, the mother of two toddlers who also has been a photojournalist and studied to be a nurse, is still in the service industry and has been waitressing at the Modern Snack Bar for seven years. She always assures customers that the restaurant's famous grasshopper pie "doesn't contain real grasshoppers" and likes to tell "Waiter, there's a fly in my soup" jokes to amused diners.

The first thing Anilee did, aside from bringing out menus, which I forgot to do ("You're falling down on the job already," she said), was to hand me a pad on which to write down orders. Then she gave me an apron with a large pocket so I could store the pad, a pen, and whatever else (straws, napkins, extra spoons) I would need to be a competent waiter and, I fervently hoped, earn a generous tip.

"Don't forget to fill the water glasses," said Anilee, making sure that I poured water from "the side of the pitcher, not the spout" and that I turned away from my customers so I wouldn't get them wet.

"Nobody's wearing a silk dress," I pointed out.

"This is going to be a long night," Anilee murmured.

After taking orders (chicken fingers for Chloe, a Caesar salad for Lauren, a turkey sandwich for Guillaume, crab cakes for Sue, and a hamburger for me, even though I wasn't supposed to eat while working), I showed the pad to Anilee, who said, "I'll have to rewrite this so the cook and the grill chef know what you mean."

She took me to the kitchen, which is in the back, and to the grill, which is in the front, and translated my chicken scratch (which isn't on the menu) into official restaurant code.

While dinner cooked, I refilled the water glasses, not only for my table (B10), but for the nice couple, Lois and Barry, at the next table ("This is the best water I've ever tasted!" Lois exclaimed) and for three women, Karen, Carol, and Karen, at another table.

"We love you!" Carol said.

"Yes," agreed one of the Karens. "But you really have to pick up the pace."

Soon, dinner was ready. I didn't dare try to balance all those plates on my arm for fear that I'd create a scene worthy of the Three Stooges, so I brought them out, one in each hand, and placed them on the table.

"Boneless appetit!" I said.

Then I sat down to eat and remarked on the good service. Because it's not polite to talk with your mouth full, nobody agreed.

Later, I brought out dessert, which included grasshopper pie for Sue and Lauren (I repeated Anilee's joke, but again there was no response) and ice cream for Chloe, who chirped, "Thank you, Poppie!"

At least she appreciated my efforts.

So, actually, did Sue, Lauren, and Guillaume, who acknowledged that I tried my best. Sue even left me a nice tip, which went into the till for Anilee and the other servers, all of whom work hard and are unfailingly cheerful and efficient.

"You may need a little more training," Anilee said when my shift was over, "but you didn't do a bad job."

"And we're still in business," said John Wittmeier, who with his brother, Otto, co-owns the Modern Snack Bar, which has been in the family since 1950. "Even you couldn't ruin us. But just to be safe," he added with a grateful smile, "don't quit your day job."

"Chloe and Poppie Make Ice Cream"

If anything is sweeter than ice cream, it's Chloe, who is sweet on ice cream herself.

That's why she was happy to meet someone who makes sweets for the sweet: Choudry Ali, who owns Magic Fountain, a popular ice cream store in Mattituck, New York.

Ali, as everybody calls him ("It's easier," he said), invited me, Chloe, and Lauren to Magic Fountain to see the magic behind the fountain of ice cream he makes every day.

"I'm going to need your help to make the next batch," Ali told Chloe, who was busy eating a cone of vanilla soft serve with sprinkles, her favorite, which Ali kindly gave to her as prepayment for her manufacturing services.

Chloe nodded, getting a dab of ice cream on her nose.

"Can I help, too?" I asked eagerly.

"Yes," Ali replied. "As long as you don't make a mess. I have a feeling that Chloe is neater than you are."

Ali, forty-nine, acknowledged that he has made his share of messes in the ten years he has owned Magic Fountain.

"One time I forgot to turn on the freezer switch, so when I opened the machine, chocolate spilled out all over the floor," Ali recalled. "I had to go home to get changed. At least I smelled good."

He was just finishing a batch of black raspberry, which prompted me to show off my vast ice cream knowledge by saying, "Let me guess. The main ingredient is black raspberry."

"What are you, a stand-up comedian?" Ali asked.

"Well, I am standing up," I noted. "If I were sitting down in a tub of black raspberry, the fruit would be on the bottom."

Lauren rolled her eyes. Chloe kept eating.

As Ali cleaned out the twenty-four-quart machine for the next batch, he said Magic Fountain has two hundred and fifty kinds of ice cream, including forty-five everyday flavors and five that rotate every two weeks.

"What's your favorite flavor?" I asked Ali.

"Pistachio," he said.

"Do you ever make extra just for yourself?" I wondered.

"Of course," he replied. "And I never get in trouble with the boss."

"My favorite is rocky road," Lauren said, adding that it helped her get through her pregnancy with Lilly.

When Ali asked what my favorite flavor is, I said, "Whatever we're about to make."

It was honey-cinnamon.

"An excellent choice," I told Ali as he opened a forty-eight-ounce bottle of honey and asked me to pour it into a plastic container.

As I squeezed, with minimal results, I asked Chloe to lend a hand, which at this point was streaked with vanilla ice cream and sprinkles. Lauren wiped it off so Chloe could help me. The honey came pouring out.

"Good job!" Lauren said.

"She's a pro," Ali added.

"How about me?" I asked.

Ali responded, "Let's just say it's a good thing Chloe is here."

Chloe smiled and helped me pour eight ounces of ground cinnamon into a measuring cup, which we then dumped into the container. Ali gave me a spatula and asked me to mix the two ingredients. I was slower than molasses, which wasn't even in there, so Ali took over and showed me how it's done, after which the honey-cinnamon had the smooth, creamy consistency of honey-cinnamon.

Ali opened the slot in the front of the machine and squeezed in a two-and-a-half-gallon bag of ice cream mix, which includes butterfat but is egg- and gluten-free, and asked me to pour in the honey-cinnamon mixture.

"Turn on the machine," Ali said. "And don't forget the freezer switch."

Twenty minutes later, the ice cream was finished. It filled two buckets totaling five gallons.

"OK," Ali said. "Time to taste it."

He handed a small plastic spoon to Chloe, who scooped some out, put it in her mouth, and exclaimed, "Wow!"

"Is it good?" Ali asked.

"Yes!" Chloe chirped.

"And you helped make it," Lauren said proudly.

"I know," said Chloe, who got a clean spoon and had another taste, after which Ali gave her a cup of vanilla and pistachio "for being such a good ice cream maker."

It was a sweet gesture by a sweet man, who gave some honey-cinnamon to Lauren and me and tried it himself. We all agreed it was great. Then Ali put the batch in the shocker, or deep freezer, where it would stay for twelve hours before being sold.

As we were leaving, Chloe gave Ali a high-five and said, "Thank you!"

"You're welcome," Ali replied. "Now you can say you taught your grandfather how to make ice cream."

"Nutty but Nice"

I work for peanuts. This may explain why I did two very important things:

(a) I bought a Powerball ticket.

(b) I made my own peanut butter.

My love of money, which I don't have much of because I had to take a vow of poverty when I went into journalism, is exceeded only by my love of peanut butter, which doesn't cost much and tastes a lot better, especially if you are the kind of person who puts his money where his mouth is.

I got the idea to make my own peanut butter when I read an online article about various uses for the stuff, which are not, apparently, limited to eating.

For instance, it can be used as shaving cream. I had never thought of this, mainly because I would rather eat peanut butter and save my shaving cream for pies, just like the Three Stooges did when they started pie fights.

Hungry for knowledge, I tried it. I got a knife and spread the peanut butter on my face, then I grabbed my trusty razor and, cheek by jowl, carefully smoothed out the situation. It worked like a charm. I didn't have razor stubble. And I didn't cut myself, though I'm sure the peanut butter would have stanched the blood.

Best of all, I smelled good, which is another use for peanut butter. According to the article, it is an odor eliminator. In addition, it's a squeak eliminator that can be used in place of WD-40 on hinges and drawers. It's also a squeak eliminator because it can be used as mouse trap bait.

Other peanut butter uses: windshield cleaner (it removes bug carcasses, which would make creamy peanut butter chunky); hair moisturizer (if you leave it in, I guess it would get rid of the gray, too); and leather cleaner (too kinky to think about).

But since the best use for peanut butter is eating, I decided to make my own.

Following a recipe I also got online, I bought a bag of raw peanuts and a bottle of peanut oil, which are the main ingredients, along with kosher salt, a box of which was already in a kitchen cabinet.

According to the instructions, I needed a food processor, a baking sheet, a spatula, and a container with a lid.

Sue, also a peanut butter fan (she likes chunky, while I prefer creamy), set up the food processor and said, "Good luck. And don't forget to clean everything up when you're done."

The most labor-intensive part of the process was shelling two cups of peanuts, some of which I ate, which is why it took about half an hour.

Then I spread them on the baking sheet, set the oven at three hundred and fifty degrees, and put them in for ten minutes, after which I dumped them into the food processor and checked out the instructions, which said, "If you toasted your nuts, do this while they are still warm. Pulse a few times until chopped."

It hurt just reading this.

Next, I ran the food processor for one minute, stopped and scraped the sides and the bottom of the bowl, and repeated the process twice. Then I put in half a teaspoon of kosher salt and two tablespoons of peanut oil and ran the processor for two more minutes.

I carefully lifted the lid, hoping my peanut butter wouldn't be like spackle. To my amazement, it had a perfectly creamy consistency. I dipped in a spoon, which I like to use when I eat the store-bought stuff straight from the jar, and lifted it to my mouth.

My taste buds did backflips. I didn't because I figured I would break something, like the food processor or my leg, but I can honestly say it was the best peanut butter I have ever tasted.

"Wow!" Sue exclaimed when I gave her some. "This is really good."

Even Maggie the dog loved it, though she had a tough time getting it off the roof of her mouth.

I spooned the peanut butter into a container and put it in the refrigerator, proud that it is too good to use as a windshield cleaner or a hair moisturizer. I won't even shave with it.

I'll just be happy that I have won the culinary equivalent of Powerball and put my peanut butter where my mouth is.

"All in Good Taste"

As a seasoned gourmand (I am usually seasoned with oregano because I am no sage), I know enough about food to give expert advice on which wine goes with Slim Jims (red) and which goes with Twinkies (white).

In fact, I have always had a burning desire, which sometimes happens in the kitchen, to be a restaurant critic. And I got my chance when I went out with a real restaurant critic to review an eatery where I passed judgment on the menu, which wasn't edible (too chewy) but did contain lots of tasty offerings.

The restaurant was Tra'mici, a cozy Italian spot in Massapequa Park, New York, and the critic was Melissa McCart, who has written sparkling reviews for the Pittsburgh Post-Gazette and Newsday. Accompanying us on this gastronomic adventure was Janelle Griffith, a talented feature writer for Newsday.

Our waiter was Marco Gervasi, who introduced himself by saying he would be our waiter (these formalities are very important in the service experience) and commented that there was an empty fourth seat at our table.

"Sit down," I urged him. "Are you hungry?" I got up, put a white cloth napkin over my arm, and said, "I'm Jerry. I'll be your waiter."

I could tell by the look in Marco's eye (his other eye was blank) that he knew he was in for a long night.

Then he asked if we wanted anything to drink. Melissa and Janelle ordered white wine, even though Twinkies were not among the entrees.

"I'll have a glass of red," I said.

"How about a cab?" Marco asked.

"If I drink enough of them," I answered, "I'll have to hail a cab for the ride home."

Marco, who looked like he could use a drink himself, smiled and dutifully went away.

He returned shortly afterward with not only our wine but a plate of hors d'oeuvres, which contained not horses (pardon my French) but salami, prosciutto, and cheese, along with olives. They tickled the palate. I soothed the tickle with a sip of wine. It was fragrant but not haughty. And vice versa.

For the main course, Melissa ordered Orecchiette alla Barese, served with broccoli rabe and sausage, and Janelle ordered Fettuccine al doppio burro, which did not (pardon my Italian) contain a stupid donkey.

When I expressed interest in a steak, Marco suggested Filetto (filet mignon with mashed potatoes, broccoli rabe, and red wine reduction).

"The meat is cured," he noted.

"Cured?" I said nervously. "What was wrong with it?"

"I can't tell you," Marco replied.

I ordered it anyway.

When our dinners came out, all three of us daintily dug in. Then we tried each other's meals, which is how restaurant critics get a taste of several menu items in one sitting (it's not a good idea to stand while eating) and can determine what's good and, in some cases, what isn't.

After Melissa sampled my steak, she said, "Yours is the winner."

"Umph, umph, umph," I agreed, even though it's not polite to talk with your mouth full of food.

This shared tasting must be done inconspicuously or the restaurant staff will suspect that a critic is in the house. In fact, Marco asked me, "What do you do?"

"As little as possible," I told him.

"No, really," he insisted. "What do you do?"

I looked around furtively and whispered, "I stick up restaurants."

Marco hurried away to get our dessert (salty caramel gelato) and possibly call the cops. He also must have alerted his boss, because the general manager came out to refill our water glasses.

"I'm Ben," he said.

"I'm Jerry," I responded, shaking his hand. "We should open an ice cream business."

"It's been done," Ben stated.

"Then we'll sue them," I said. "Just as soon as my lawyer gets out of jail."

"You can call it Jerry and Ben's," Janelle suggested.

Dessert was delicious, just like the rest of the meal. And the service was even better, which is saying something considering that Marco was working only his second shift at Tra'mici.

"What's your day job?" I asked him.

"I'm a real estate agent," Marco said.

"Do you get a commission on dinners?" I wondered.

"Yes," he said. "It's called a tip."

He got a generous one. After dealing with me, he deserved it, which is why I am giving Tra'mici an excellent review.

"Keep up the good work," I told Ben on the way out. "And give my compliments to the waiter."

"A Hole Lot of Fun"

Chloe is so sweet that she doesn't mind that I have a hole in my head. She's also sweet on doughnuts, most of which have holes that rival mine.

So it was only fitting that, in keeping with the old Dunkin' Donuts commercial in which Fred the Baker said, "Time to make the doughnuts," we went to Dunkin' Donuts because it was, as Chloe the Baker said, "Time to make the doughnuts."

We arrived at the Dunkin' Donuts store in Coram, New York, where Chloe and I often go so she can have her favorite doughnut (strawberry frosted with rainbow sprinkles) and I can have mine (jelly with powdered sugar), and were warmly greeted by shift leader Dinora Ramos.

"Is it time to make the doughnuts?" I asked.

"Yes," Dinora replied. "How did you know?"

"I have a hole in my head," I said.

"Doughnuts have holes, too, Poppie," Chloe told me.

"Also," I said to Dinora, "I'm half-baked."

"That's why Chloe will be making the doughnuts," said Dinora, who asked me to help Chloe wash her hands (I had to be useful somehow) and then gave her a pair of clear plastic gloves so she not only would be abiding by health standards but wouldn't get frosting and sprinkles all over her fingers, which happens when she eats doughnuts.

After donning an apron, so she wouldn't get frosting and sprinkles all over her clothes, either, Chloe stepped up on a stool and got ready to decorate a batch of bare doughnuts that sat on a counter behind the store's display case.

"These have already been made," Dinora explained, "but you can put on any kind of topping you want."

Dinora gave Chloe a spreader, which she dipped into a container of strawberry frosting. Then she spread the pink mixture over the first doughnut well enough to impress Dinora and the rest of the friendly staff.

"She's a pro," said Carlos Rivero, another shift leader.

"I use a spreader when I put spackle on the walls at home before I paint," I said.

"It's a good thing you're not making doughnuts," Carlos noted.

"That's true," I answered. "Spackle wouldn't taste too good, even with sprinkles."

"Speaking of sprinkles, would you like to put some on your doughnut?" Dinora asked Chloe, who chose the rainbow variety, which she sprinkled, very neatly, over the frosting.

"Great job, Chloe!" I said.

Chloe beamed proudly and replied, "Thank you, Poppie! Can I do another one?"

Dinora kindly let her do several more, including one for me, a jelly doughnut that Chloe topped with powdered sugar.

"Now," said Dinora, "let's go to the kitchen."

Safety rules prohibited Chloe and me from getting near the oven, but Chloe actually did make doughnuts by filling a couple of them with jelly (she pushed the button on a pump machine) and spreading powdered sugar on others.

"She could be a baker," said Johnny, one of the store's three bakers, who make about ten thousand doughnuts a day for the area's eleven stores.

After Chloe made two more jellies, we went back out front.

"You're quite a chef, Chloe," said Dinora.

"I know," Chloe replied.

"Did you have fun?" asked Dinora.

"Yes!" Chloe exclaimed.

We both thanked Dinora, who handed us two boxes of doughnuts and said, "I know they'll be really good because you made them, Chloe."

Then we drove back to Nini and Poppie's house, where Sue waited with Lauren, Guillaume, and Lilly.

Chloe's creations ran the gamut from vanilla to chocolate to jelly to Boston cream, topped with all kinds of sprinkles, chips, sugar, and frosting.

As we got ready to savor her delicious treats, the little baker sat at the kitchen table and, holding a strawberry frosted with rainbow sprinkles in soon-to-be-messy fingers, smiled and said, "Time to eat the doughnuts."

"How Not to Eat an Ice Cream Cone"

As a journalist, I know the importance of getting a scoop. As a grandfather, I know the importance of getting two scoops.

That's what I learned when I took Chloe to McNulty's Ice Cream Parlor in Miller Place, New York, for a lesson in how to eat an ice cream cone.

Chloe and I have eaten ice cream together many times, whether it has been at a store like McNulty's or at the ice cream truck that makes my house a regular stop on its appointed rounds through the neighborhood.

(God, now I can't get that annoying jingle out of my head!)

But the two of us had always eaten our ice cream out of cups, which is nice and relatively neat but not very challenging for those hardy souls who like to risk a spectacular cleaning bill while licking, slurping, or otherwise inhaling a cone before the ice cream drips all over your hands, your clothes, your shoes, your seat, the table, the floor, or, if you are not careful, everything and everyone within a radius of approximately a hundred yards.

"I want a cone, Poppie," Chloe said as we entered McNulty's and perused the display case, which was stocked with so many varieties that it was a veritable explosion of colors.

"What flavor, Chloe?" I asked.

"Strawberry, please, Poppie," Chloe answered politely.

I passed her order to server Kelsey Reynolds, eighteen, who inquired, "One scoop or two?"

I looked down at Chloe, who was holding my hand. She looked up at me and beamed. It melted my heart faster than a bowl of sherbet during a heat wave.

"Two," I said.

Kelsey handed me the ice cream cone equivalent of the Empire State Building. I conjured a mess of immense proportions. That likely possibility doubled when I ordered a similarly lofty cone of vanilla soft serve for myself.

"May I have some napkins?" I asked Kelsey, who gave me four. "We're going to need a lot more than that," I said.

Kelsey nodded knowingly and gave me another dozen.

"Enjoy!" she said as Chloe and I headed to a table, where we sat down and commenced cone consumption.

I tried to impress upon Chloe the importance of eating her ice cream around the edges before it began its slow descent onto the cone and, immediately thereafter, her fingers.

Unfortunately, she didn't heed this brilliant advice. Also unfortunately, neither did I. My soft serve, temporarily neglected as I was giving a lecture in the fine if somewhat sticky art of eating an ice cream cone, began to seep under my fingernails.

"Do you need more napkins?" asked Kelsey, who saw that the lesson was not going well and came over to offer assistance.

And not a moment too soon. That's because Chloe took a bite out of the bottom of her cone, causing a virtual Niagara of strawberry ice cream to pour onto the table, as well as the sleeve of her pink sweater. At least the colors blended.

Then she placed her cone on the saturated blanket of napkins that covered the table and asked to try my cone, with strikingly similar results.

I knew I had failed completely when Chloe looked at my cream-covered digits and declared, "Poppie is sloppy!"

Kelsey must have agreed because she brought over even more napkins.

"Don't worry," she said sympathetically as I mopped up the tabletop, "I've seen worse."

But the lesson was ultimately successful because Chloe and I had a sweet time. It took a while, but we both finished our cones.

After we washed our hands in the bathroom, it was time to go.

"Thank you," I said to Kelsey on the way out.

"You're very welcome," she replied with a bright smile. "Next time you and Chloe come in, call ahead. I want to make sure we have enough napkins."

5

"Health Hath No Fury"

"The Skin Game"

For the past forty years, which is how long I have been in journalism, I have had a nose for news. So I guess it was not surprising that the news I received recently involved my nose.

Who knows what news you will receive about your nose until you go to the dermatologist, which is what I did and was told I had skin cancer on — you guessed it — my ear.

No, actually, it was on my nose, which is my most prominent feature with the notable exception of my mouth, a cavelike aperture that should be featured in National Geographic.

But back to my nose, which is nothing to sneeze at.

"I think I know what this is," said my dermatologist, Dr. Adam Korzenko, who has a practice in Port Jefferson Station, New York.

"Yes," I replied helpfully, "it's my nose. Believe it or not, it was this size when I was born. I couldn't lift my head until I was three years old."

"No," the good doctor told his patient patiently, "I mean this little red spot."

"In my case," I countered, "the red spot isn't so little. If I stood on a street corner, cars might actually stop."

"I am going to do a biopsy," Dr. Korzenko said, "but I am ninety-nine percent sure this is a basal cell carcinoma. It's not life-threatening, but you should have it removed."

"My nose?" I exclaimed. "That would involve dynamite and jackhammers. You'd have to hire a construction crew."

"You can keep your nose," Dr. Korzenko said reassuringly.

"Good," I responded, "because nobody else would want it. But I have to ask a question: How could I have skin cancer? I am not a sun worshipper. And if I go out on a sunny day, I always slather myself with sunscreen."

"This probably goes back to when you were a kid," Dr. Korzenko said. "It's very common. I see eight hundred cases a year. And it's really nothing to worry about. But you should have it taken care of."

The skin, Dr. Korzenko said, is the body's largest organ (sorry, guys), which is why it is important to have it checked regularly.

A few days later, the biopsy came back positive.

"Are you positive?" I asked the nice person who called with the news.

"Yes," she said. "We'll book you with a surgeon."

Not long afterward, I went to East Setauket, New York, and sat in the office of Dr. Evan Jones, who was ready to do a Mohs procedure.

"Mohs?" I inquired. "Please tell me Larry and Curly won't be assisting."

"They're on vacation," said Dr. Jones, adding that he would numb my nose with a local anesthetic.

"I don't care where it comes from," I said. "You could even use something imported, like beer. I could go for one."

"Then," he explained, "I'll take off a thin layer and run a test on it. If I need to take off another layer, I will until there are no more cancer cells."

The procedure lasted about an hour, most of it spent waiting for the results to come back. Dr. Jones took off one layer and a tiny bit more before saying, "OK, you're all done."

The next day, I went to see Dr. Gregory Diehl, a plastic surgeon in Port Jefferson Station.

"I don't want to end up with a third nostril," I told him.

"You can breathe easy with two nostrils," he said.

"Maybe you can use spackle," I suggested. "Of course, then you'd have to throw in the trowel."

"I have a better way," said Dr. Diehl, who explained how he would take skin from the upper right side of my nose and use it to seamlessly cover the cancerous area that was removed during the Mohs procedure.

It was ingenious. And artistic. And swell, even though my nose didn't swell any more than it did before.

Now I am cancer-free, on the mend, and looking as lovely as ever. And I owe it to Drs. Korzenko, Jones, and Diehl, all of whom are credits to their profession and good guys to boot.

I may not be a doctor myself, but I am going to give everyone a prescription: Go to the dermatologist regularly and wear sunscreen.

The nose knows.

"The Cool Cat in the Hat"

I have never been a man of many hats, not just because I am afraid I'd get stuck in doorways, but because my head, though empty, is too big to fit even one hat over.

But that changed when, after a bout with skin cancer on my nose, which is attached to my head and is almost as big, I was urged by my dermatologist to buy a hat.

"Get one with a wide brim," he suggested. "It will keep the sun off your head — remember, the rays can penetrate your hair — and will protect your face, including your nose."

"To cover my whole nose," I replied, "I'd need a sombrero. Or a beach umbrella."

"A regular hat will do," my dermatologist said. "But get one."

So, for the first time in my life, I went hat shopping. To make sure I didn't buy anything that would make me look even dumber than I already do, I brought along Sue, who likes hats and has great style. I, unfortunately, have a fashion plate in my head.

"What kind of hat do you want?" Sue asked.

"I don't know," I said. "I've never worn one."

What I didn't want was a baseball cap. I haven't played baseball in half a century. And even then I was awful. Plus, to conform to a look adopted by just about every guy who wears a baseball cap these days, I'd have to put it on backward, which would assure, at least, that I wouldn't get skin cancer on the back of my neck.

Sue and I went to three stores and all we could find were — you guessed it — beach umbrellas.

No, I mean baseball caps.

Then we spotted a mall store called Tilly's.

"This place is for young people," Sue noted as we walked in.

"I'm young," I countered. "At least in my head. And since I need to cover it with a hat, I guess we're in the right place."

Indeed we were because the store had all kinds of hats.

The first one I saw was a straw hat with a brim as wide as my shoulders. Naturally, it didn't fit over my head.

"One size fits all," said a young (of course) salesperson named Dana.

"You mean one size fits all except me," I replied. "Do you have a measuring tape so you can see how tremendous my head is?"

"No," she said, spying my cranium and trying not to imply that the tape would have to be as long as the first-down chains in a football game.

Sue and I walked to the back of the store, where I saw a felt hat with a wide brim and a band. I tried it on. Incredibly, it fit.

"I look like Indiana Jones," I told a salesperson named James after seeing myself in a mirror.

"You're a lot younger than the guy who plays him," he said, referring to Harrison Ford, who looks great in a hat.

"I'm going to get a feather," Sue chimed in, "and stick it in the band."

"Then I'd look like Super Fly," I said.

"Cool," said James, giving me two thumbs-up.

On the way out, I saw another hat, a khaki boonie that made me look like Bill Murray in "Caddyshack."

"This one fits, too," I said in amazement. "And the brim covers my nose."

A salesperson named Anna smiled but was too polite to comment, except to say, "It looks good."

Sue agreed.

"Now you have a hat to wear when you get dressed up and one for lounging around outside," she said at the register, where we paid a grand total of twenty-five dollars for both.

"You know what they say," I noted. "Two hats are better than one."

"Papa Had Another Stone"

It may come as a shock to you that I can't get pregnant. The reason, of course, is that I am too old. But that did not stop a doctor from sending me for a sonogram.

This procedure, which is often performed on pregnant women, was done on me, not because I was expecting a baby, unlikely since I am still infantile myself, but because I had a kidney stone.

Unfortunately, it wasn't my first. It was my fifth. Or sixth. I have lost count, mostly under the influence of painkilling drugs, but I do know that I am a human quarry who manufactures these things at an alarming rate. If I could outsource this manufacturing to another person, I would. But I can't, so I continue to have kidney stones.

The first time I had one, a nurse told me it was the male equivalent of childbirth. I told her that at least I wouldn't have to put the stone through college.

This time, my urologist, Dr. Albert Kim, who has a practice in the appropriately named New York hamlet of Stony Brook, ordered a sonogram because I'd already had enough X-rays from my previous kidney stones to glow in the dark, which at least would reduce my electric bills.

When I arrived at Zwanger-Pesiri Radiology, I spoke with Amy, one of the nice people who work at the front desk.

"I've been here so often that I should have my own parking space," I told her.

"Even I can't get one," Amy said with a smile. Then she handed me paperwork whose sheer volume rivaled that of "War and Peace" and asked me to fill it out.

"I've had to do this so many times that my right hand should be X-rayed," I said.

Amy nodded sympathetically and replied, "You can keep the pen."

Then I was called in by a nice technologist named Erin, who asked if I had been drinking.

"No," I replied, "but I could go for a beer."

"I mean water," Erin said. "You have to have at least twenty-four ounces before we can do a sonogram."

"I had a bottle on the way over," I told her.

"Good," said Erin, who asked me to lift my shirt so she could rub some jelly on my belly and watch it on the telly.

"Am I pregnant?" I asked.

"Sorry," she responded, "but no."

"Do you see my kidney stone?" I wondered.

"I'm not a doctor," Erin explained, "so I'm not allowed to say."

But she did say that a report would be sent to Dr. Kim, with whom I had an appointment the next day. That evening, however, someone from the radiology center called me at home to say I had to come back because part of the sonogram was blurred.

The next morning, I returned for another one. While I was waiting, I had a kidney stone attack. Fortunately, it was no worse than having hot tar injected into my right side. When the pain subsided, I had a second sonogram and then went to see Dr. Kim, who said the stone was probably dropping and that this, too, shall pass.

Sure enough, at home later that afternoon, it did. Dr. Kim ordered an X-ray, which I tried to avoid in the first place.

I had one a couple of days later from another nice technologist named Jenn, who said I could keep the blue paper pants I had to wear for the procedure. She also gave me a copy of the X-ray, which I had to bring to Dr. Kim a few days later.

I also brought him the stone, which looked to be the size of a bocce ball but was actually, according to Dr. Kim, five or six millimeters.

"It's fairly big," he said. "Did you have a tough time passing it?"

"It wasn't pleasant, but it could have been worse," I replied. "At least I didn't have a baby."

"Tooth or Consequences"

In one of my favorite Three Stooges shorts, the boys are dentists. When their first patient comes in, Shemp puts on a pair of Coke bottle glasses that render him practically sightless. Then he pries open the hapless man's mouth, grabs a pair of pliers, and, while Moe reads instructions from a book titled "Carpentry Made Easy," proceeds to extract a tooth in a painfully funny scene that makes me glad I don't have a dentist like that.

So you can imagine how I felt when I walked into my new dentist's office for my initial appointment and saw, on the TV in the waiting area, an episode of — you guessed it — the Three Stooges.

"They are my heroes," said Dr. Anthony Fazio, who was not, thank God, wielding pliers, a hammer, or any other tool the Stooges might have used to treat a patient on his very first visit.

"I save those for subsequent visits," added Dr. Fazio, who doesn't need to use laughing gas because his delightfully skewed sense of humor puts patients at ease and actually makes it fun to go to the dentist.

Dr. Fazio, who wears glasses ("Where are you?" he joked after I had settled into the chair), has been clowning with patients since he opened his practice in Medford, New York, in 1998.

"I took over from Dr. William J. Tinkler, who's eighty-eight and is a funny guy himself," said Dr. Fazio, adding that Dr. Tinkler was his dental school teacher at Stony Brook University, where Dr. Fazio now teaches. "We put on a show every year at the school and Dr. Tinkler gets up and tells jokes. He's another one of my heroes."

Dr. Fazio, forty-six, is married to Dr. Lynn Travis, herself a Stony Brook dental school graduate.

"We put down roots in the community," he deadpanned.

"You know the drill," I responded.

"You shouldn't have said that," countered Dr. Fazio, who, fortunately for me, didn't need to use one.

But he did need to regale me with stories of his dental adventures, such as the one he called "The Ventriloquist and His Wife."

"The patient was this very stately gentleman," Dr. Fazio recalled. "I asked him what I could do for him and, without missing a beat, his wife said, 'He hates his teeth and needs new dentures.' I asked the man what he didn't like about them and his wife said, 'He doesn't like the color. And he can't chew with them.' Whatever I asked the man, his wife answered. Then I said to him, 'That's amazing.' He was puzzled. I said, 'You are the best ventriloquist I've ever seen.' There was a hint of a smile on his face.

"I priced a new set of dentures at two thousand dollars. Then I asked the wife if she would be in the room during the treatment and she said, 'Of course.' So I said in that case, the dentures would be four thousand dollars. I said, 'If I have to talk with your husband and you, it will cost double.' She got huffy and said, 'I never!' On the way out, her husband said to me, 'Have a nice day.' It was the only time I heard him speak."

Then there was the young woman who practically did a burlesque routine in the office.

"She was very attractive," Dr. Fazio said. "I had to check out her occlusion, so I took a piece of typing paper, placed it between her teeth, and said, 'Would you please grind for me?' She started to gyrate in the chair. I said, 'No, no, no! I meant that you should grind your teeth from side to side.' She started to laugh and said, 'Sorry, I thought it was an odd request, but you're kind of cute and I figured, what the hell, why not?' She's still one of my best patients."

I could never compete with her, but Dr. Fazio said I'm now a good patient, too.

"You're memorable," he noted.

Maybe it's because I share his appreciation for old movies, posters for which fill the walls. One of the films is "Dial M for Murder."

"The M doesn't also stand for molar, does it?" I asked tremulously.

"No," Dr. Fazio said after hygienist Margaret Skladanek had done a terrific job of cleaning my teeth and office manager Lisa Rugen had set up my next appointment. "But it could stand for Moe."

As I left the office, the Three Stooges were still on.

"At least you don't have any carpentry books in here," I said.

"I'll get one in time for your next visit," Dr. Fazio replied. "Nyuk, nyuk, nyuk!"

"Worth the Weight"

As a one-hundred-seventy-five-pound weakling whose idea of lifting weights is doing twelve-ounce curls, I had always vowed that I would never go to any gym that wasn't situated next to a bar.

I found such an unlikely combination when I won a one-day trial membership to Blink Fitness, which has gyms in New York, New Jersey, Pennsylvania, and California.

Because going to the West Coast would entail hopping on a plane, a form of exercise frowned upon by the Federal Aviation Administration, I drove to the Blink location in Melville, New York, which happens to be situated next to Blackstone Steakhouse, an establishment that has a bar where powerlifters such as myself can do twelve-ounce curls.

My brief membership began after work, where I didn't work up much of a sweat, and ended an hour and a half later in the upstairs equipment room, where I didn't work up much of a sweat, either, because I was too busy talking to members who were trying to work up a sweat but couldn't because, of course, I was talking to them.

"How's it going?" I asked Scott Grimando, forty-eight, an illustrator who was in the middle of a workout on the shoulder press machine.

"OK," Scott replied between huffs and puffs. "Trying to keep in shape."

Except for a woman who was working out with a personal trainer and appeared to be even older than I am (sixty-three physically, eight mentally), Scott was one of the more senior members, most of whom appeared to be in their twenties and already in such good shape that they shouldn't have bothered working out.

"I have a one-day membership," I told Scott.

"Make the most of it," he said, adding that he's a pescatarian.

"I'm Catholic," I responded. "And I may need last rites before the night is out."

Scott patiently explained that a pescatarian is a person who doesn't eat meat but does eat fish. "It's a good diet to be on," he said, returning to his shoulder presses.

I sat down next to him and did ten at a weight that probably didn't exceed that of a Chihuahua on a pescatarian diet.

Next I spoke with David Kahn, fifty, a lawyer who was on a pedal machine.

"I want to look buff," said David, who did. "Also, I got hurt Rollerblading, so coming to the gym is safer."

David, who used to play soccer and softball, practices corporate law and said he couldn't represent me if I got hurt working out.

"But I could represent the gym," he said with a smile.

"In that case," I said, "I'll take it easy on the machines."

And I was on plenty of them. There was the treadmill (where I watched Charlie Sheen in a rerun of "Two and a Half Men"); the moving stairs (which I climbed steadily but didn't get anywhere); the calf exerciser (I didn't see any livestock); and the dumbbells (I was the biggest one).

All in all, it was an invigorating experience. The gym was clean and spacious, the people were friendly, and the equipment was top-notch. And I didn't need last rites.

"How was it?" assistant manager Christian Dellosso, twenty-three, asked as I was leaving.

"Terrific," I said. "Considering I'm forty years older than you are, I feel really good."

"Great," Christian said. "I hope you'll join."

"I'm thinking about it," I said. "But first, I have to go next door for one more workout."

I strolled over to Blackstone Steakhouse and ordered a beer from bartender Vinny Fodera, fifty-nine, who sported a sweeping mustache and a muscular build.

"Do you work out?" I asked.

"No," Vinny said. "I used to lift weights, but they were too heavy."

"If you don't mind," I said, lifting a cold one, "I'm going to do some twelve-ounce curls."

"Be my guest," Vinny said. "For guys our age, it's the best exercise you can get."

"CPR for Dummies"

When it comes to saving lives, I used to be such a dummy that I couldn't even spell CPR. Then I took a CPR class in which the instructor used me as a dummy. Now I am a lifesaver. And if you're ever choking on one, I can save your life.

I was transformed from a nervous wreck who knew only the Heineken maneuver ("You're choking? Have a beer!") to a confident guy who also knows the Heimlich ("Pop goes the Life Saver!") by Tom Henry, the dashing, funny, extremely impressive trainer who taught the CPR class I took at work.

I was among seventeen aspiring heroes in the auditorium, where Tom had assembled the tools of his trade: masks, defibrillators, and, of course, dummies, of which I would be the biggest.

"These mannequins and dolls are my second family, except they don't talk back," said Tom, fifty-five, a former New York City CSI detective ("It was boring compared to the TV show," he acknowledged) who now runs an American Heart Association-approved CPR training center.

The mannequins and dolls came in three sizes: adult, child, and baby. Since the adults were only heads and torsos, Tom wanted to demonstrate on a real-life dummy.

"Jerry!" he said, pointing in my direction. "Come on up."

I bounded to the middle of the spacious room and was asked to lie on the floor, next to an adult mannequin.

Tom gazed down and said, "The dummy is better-looking."

Then he ran through the possibilities of why I might need CPR, among them a heart attack or a bad fall.

"If I hit my head," I said, "I wouldn't get hurt."

"I can see why," said Tom, adding that one of the first things to do is to take off the victim's shirt in case a defibrillator is needed. "I am NOT going to take off Jerry's shirt," he announced.

My colleagues, both men and women, breathed an audible sigh of relief.

Tom then said mouth-to-mouth resuscitation might be needed.

"Am I going to lock lips with Jerry?" he asked. "No way!"

Instead, he demonstrated the technique used in pumping the victim's chest to keep the heart beating. It didn't hurt because Tom didn't use full force — he saved that for the mannequin — but it did tickle.

When Tom was finished, he helped me up and announced, "We saved Jerry!"

My colleagues applauded, which also did my heart good, though I'm sure none of them wanted to lock lips with me, either.

"When performing CPR, you can't worry about hurting somebody," Tom said. "If a person is in cardiac arrest, they're dead. You can't make it worse. You can't hurt somebody who's dead. Although in Jerry's case," he added, "it might be difficult to tell the difference."

Later, Tom used me to demonstrate how to perform the Heimlich maneuver.

"Despite what Jerry says," he noted, "it doesn't involve beer. You have to do this if a person is choking."

Tom got behind me and put his arms around my middle, showing the class how to force out whatever might be lodged (a Wint O Green Life Saver, perhaps, or an entire Happy Meal) in my upper airway.

"You should be careful when doing this to someone who's pregnant," Tom advised.

"Don't worry," I said. "I'm not."

"No," Tom replied, "but you are kind of flabby."

We used the mannequins to learn how to perform CPR and do mouth-to-mouth resuscitation.

"If you were breathing into Jerry's mouth," Tom told my classmates, "you'd have to hope he brushed his teeth."

"I did that yesterday," I said.

The last thing we learned was how to use an AED (automated external defibrillator), which was demonstrated on a mannequin.

"We're not going to jump-start Jerry," Tom said. "He's been through enough today."

But it was well worth it. The three-hour class was fun, fascinating, and vital. And Tom was a great instructor.

"You were great, too," he said when the session was over. "In fact, when it comes to CPR, you're a real dummy."

"Nothing but the Tooth"

If I were a lawyer — which I always thought I should be because I have been admitted to the bar many times — I'd have a retainer.

I'm not a lawyer — because I have been thrown out of the bar many times, too — but I have a retainer anyway.

I refer not to the advance fee a lawyer gets so he or she can pay the bar tab, but to the device that holds your teeth in place so you will have a nice smile when addressing a jury or, in my case (the People v. Zezima), pleading not guilty to Larceny, Chicanery & Mopery, attorneys at law, for failing to pay the bar tab.

"You need a new retainer," said Dr. Ammar Alsamawi, a third-year resident at the Stony Brook University School of Dental Medicine. "If I give you one, you could be my lawyer."

"If you want me to be your lawyer," I said, "I'd advise you to plead insanity."

Dr. Alsamawi, twenty-nine, who was born and raised in Iraq and immigrated to the United States almost nine years ago, is a third-year resident at Stony Brook, where I had undergone a lengthy but happily successful treatment to straighten two teeth that had been knocked out of alignment by the foot that's usually in my mouth.

When the treatment concluded a few years ago, I got retainers. Unfortunately, the top retainer recently cracked and one of the teeth, a lateral incisor, was beginning to turn back out of alignment.

"I have to rotate it," Dr. Alsamawi said.

"You mean like a mechanic rotates tires?" I asked. "Will you have to put me on a lift in a garage?"

"No, you can stay in the chair," the good doctor replied. "And I won't even give you an oil change."

But he did make impressions of all my teeth, top and bottom, and said he would see me the following week to apply my new retainers.

When I went back, I greeted Dr. Alsamawi by pronouncing his last name correctly.

"I've been practicing all week," I said.

"Wow," he replied. "That's a real skill. Most of my colleagues still can't pronounce my name. But I'm impressed that you practiced. You have too much time on your hands."

"On my feet, too," I said as I propped them up on the chair and leaned back so Dr. Alsamawi, which I couldn't pronounce this time because my mouth was wide open, could fit the new retainers over my baby grand piano keys.

"Did I make a good impression?" I inquired after he snapped them into place.

"You mean did I make a good impression?" said Dr. Alsamawi, adding that he made the clear retainers in a small laboratory at the school.

"They fit like a glove," I noted.

"That's because I was wearing gloves when I made them," said Dr. Alsamawi, whose own teeth are perfectly straight.

"Did you ever have braces?" I asked.

"Yes," he answered. "I just got done with my treatment a year ago."

Like me, Dr. Alsamawi had Invisalign, the brand name for what are commonly known as invisible braces.

"You know the worst thing about them?" I said.

"What?" he replied.

"You can't find them."

"Why?"

"Because," I said triumphantly, "they're invisible."

Dr. Alsamawi flashed a Hollywood smile.

"You could be a movie star," I said.

His handsome visage blushed as he said modestly, "I'm no movie star."

"If this orthodontic gig doesn't work out," I suggested, "you should get an agent."

"You don't want me to leave before your incisor is straightened out, do you?" he said.

"No!" I exclaimed. "You're going to get me on the straight and narrow. Or, in the case of my mouth, the straight and wide."

Dr. Alsamawi explained that incisors are the "meanest, most annoying teeth" because they have "a mind of their own."

"That's more than I can say for myself," I said.

"Keep the retainers on about eighteen hours a day for six weeks," Dr. Alsamawi said. "By then, your incisor will have taken a good turn."

"As your lawyer," I told him, "I can say without fear of prosecution that one good turn deserves another."

6

"Kid Stuff"

"The Kids Are All Right"

When I became a grandfather almost four years ago, I learned that babysitting is child's play: As long as you play with the child, are willing to do diaper duty, and don't confuse the kid's bottle with your own, you can be a great grandfather.

But what would happen if you had two grandchildren — one preschooler and one infant — to babysit?

That's the situation in which I found myself when Lauren, Guillaume, and Sue all went out of town and left me, for the first time, to watch both girls.

Here is a record of the marathon.

5:30 a.m.: The alarm clock goes off and I bound out of bed, stubbing my toe on the radiator. I am off and limping.

5:45: Sue and Lauren finish packing. They won't be back until Sunday. Guillaume, who already has been gone for three days, isn't scheduled to return for another twelve hours. To show how challenging child care is, I am the only alternative. At least my services don't cost anything.

6:15: Chloe gets up. We immediately start playing. This will go on all day.

6:40: Sue and Lauren leave for the airport. Bon voyage!

6:45: Lilly wakes up. I bring her downstairs in her Rock 'n Play Sleeper and wish there was something like that for adults. It would be great to drink beer in.

7:00: Chloe and I make a delicious breakfast of scrambled eggs and sausage without burning the house down.

7:45: I give Lilly a bottle. It contains formula. (See 6:45 entry.)

8:30: Sue calls from the airport to make sure everything is OK. "I have to go," I tell her. "The first responders are here." Sue sighs and hangs up.

9:15: Lilly poops! She hadn't done so for three days and her deposit is, to put it mildly, breathtaking. Not to be outdone, Chloe announces she has to go potty. Then Maggie the dog has to go out. The girls are firing on all cylinders.

9:30: While Lilly naps, Chloe and I amuse ourselves by running around the house and generally acting silly. It would be hard to tell who is babysitting whom.

11:00: I dress the girls, Chloe in a nice outfit Lauren picked out and Lilly in a onesie. I get dressed in a twosie (sweatshirt and sweatpants) but forget, I realize later that night, to brush my teeth.

11:45: Lilly has another bottle. This kid is starting to rival me in my college days.

12:30 p.m.: Chloe and I have peanut butter and jelly sandwiches for lunch. Chloe gets some on her new white sweater. I try to get it off with dishwashing liquid. Then I stick the sweater in the bottom of the girls' laundry pile and hope nobody notices.

1:30: Since it is a beautiful day, all of us go outside. Chloe blows bubbles, Lilly enjoys the fresh air, and Maggie fertilizes the lawn. Miraculously, nobody steps in it.

2:30: We go back inside and continue playing.

3:15: Lilly has yet another bottle.

3:30: Lauren calls to say she and Sue have landed and to see if we are still alive. I tell her that I am burping Lilly. I also tell her not to worry because I have everything under control. Then I burp. Lauren sighs and hangs up.

4:30: I put on Chloe's favorite TV program, "The Mr. Men Show," which is now my favorite, too.

6:15: Lilly gulps down her fourth bottle. Afterward, I change her diaper, which is wet enough to fill a kiddie pool.

7:00: Guillaume returns from his overseas trip but is too tired to eat and falls asleep in a chair. Chloe and I have leftover stuffed peppers for dinner. Then I give her a bath and put her to bed.

8:00: I put Guillaume to bed (he can take his own bath) and stay up with Lilly.

11:45: Lilly has a fifth. I have a glass of wine. Then we both hit the sack. It's been a great day. Guillaume is impressed the following morning. So are Sue and Lauren when they get back on Sunday.

"The girls were as good as gold," I tell them. "And I'm twice as great a grandfather as I was before."

"The Life (and Almost Death) of the Party"

For a geezer like me, it's nice to go to a birthday party that isn't your own because you don't have to put up with wisecracks about needing a fire extinguisher to blow out the candles.

Then again, when there are only four candles, you can blow them out yourself without going into cardiac arrest.

That's the lesson I learned fifty-nine years ago but forgot until recently, when I accompanied Chloe, who will soon be four herself, to a birthday party for her preschool classmate Mason, whose celebration was at a children's activity center where I climbed, slid, bounced, crawled, ran around, and otherwise worked up such a sweat that I almost went into cardiac arrest anyway.

I knew I was in for an intense experience that might end in an ambulance ride when I walked in with Chloe and was told by the nice young woman at the desk that Mason's party wouldn't start for an hour. She gave me a day pass, asked that Chloe and I take off our shoes, and said we and the fifteen other kids and their parents (I was the only grandparent) could have the run of the place until the festivities officially began.

And run we did. First, Chloe took me to a giant rubber slide that was so high it would have made a mountain goat dizzy. I am not a mountain goat (my ears are too short), but I am naturally dizzy, so I was in my element. Upon reaching the top, I held Chloe's hand and we whooshed down at such an alarming speed that my stomach was temporarily lodged in my sinuses.

It was fun the first time we went. It was fun the second time. By approximately the dozenth time, my knees were as gelatinous as my brain.

But this was only a prelude to a maze called Kilimanjaro. I'm not sure how many preschoolers have read Hemingway, but by the time I found my way out, long after Chloe had completed the course, my limbs were so sore it was almost a farewell to arms.

My legs didn't fare much better in the inflatable castle, where I bounced with Chloe until my lungs were about to explode like the Hindenburg. ("Oh, the stupidity!") The structure flashed with multicolored lights and pulsated with tunes such as the 1965 Lesley Gore hit "It's My Party (and I'll Cry If I Want To)." It wasn't my party, but I wanted to cry when I fell out and was helped up by a sympathetic mom who asked if I was hurt.

"No," I replied. "I landed on my head."

"You're a good egg," she said.

"At this point," I noted, "I'm a scrambled egg."

Finally, mercifully, mere moments before paramedics had to be called, it was time for Mason's party, which was in a back room where the kids could giggle, the parents could converse, and I, thank God, could catch my breath.

"You're not serving beer, are you?" I asked Mason's mother, Danielle, who smiled and said, "No, but you look like you need one."

Mason's father, Gavin, added, "We have lemonade."

I had a cup. It hit the spot. And the party was fantastic. Chloe saw her friends, including Mason, of course. We all had pizza, after which there were cupcakes. When it came time to sing happy birthday to Mason, the kids gathered around and helped him blow out the candle on his cupcake. The candle was lit again so he could blow it out himself.

"Make a wish," Danielle told him.

Without missing a beat, Mason said, "I wish for money!"

He got toys instead, but the day was priceless. Everyone had a great time, including me, not just because I accompanied Chloe, but because it looks like I will live to celebrate my next birthday.

The party won't be at a children's activity center, but there will be beer. And if Chloe learns how to handle a fire extinguisher, she can help me blow out the candles.

"The Manny"

If I ever retire — with the way things are going, I'll be working posthumously — I will use my newfound freedom and heretofore undiscovered talent to do what I was apparently born to do: I'll be a full-time babysitter for my three grandchildren.

I know this is my true calling because I got a ringing endorsement from Lauren, who is the mommy of Chloe, four, and Lilly, six months, whom I have babysat many times without mess, mayhem, or mishap. Or at least without anything that couldn't be cleaned up with some sort of disinfectant.

"I vouched for you," Lauren told me after she got a call from Katie, the mommy of my new grandson, Xavier. Sue and I were about to embark on a road trip to meet the little guy and Katie wanted to know if I could be trusted to care for Xavier by myself in case she and Sue went out to shop for food, diapers, or, as a perk for being a new mother, wine.

"If I could hire Dad full time, I would," Lauren told Katie. "But I can't afford him."

I was so flattered that I offered to work for nothing, which is exactly what I am worth in my present job.

But I proved my value during the week Sue and I spent with Katie, daddy Dave, and, of course Xavier, who is beautiful, just like Chloe and Lilly.

Aside from Dave, Guillaume, and yours truly, Xavier is the only male in the immediate family, which otherwise consists of Sue, Katie, Lauren, Chloe, Lilly, and Maggie the dog, the sole surviving member of a pet population that once consisted of another dog (Lizzie) and four cats (Ramona, Kitty, Bernice, and, the only male, Henry, with whom I never really bonded).

But I more than made up for it with Xavier. Our male bonding included two a.m. feedings. I fed Xavier, too.

These sessions sometimes began as early as midnight and as late as four a.m. because Xavier hadn't developed a regular sleeping pattern, which means his parents and grandparents hadn't, either.

But it was my pleasure to stay up with him. There was giggling, snoring, burping, hiccuping, drooling, sneezing, tooting and other bodily functions common to guys of a certain age, be it three weeks or sixty-three years.

Speaking of bodily functions, you novice babysitters should know that, while boys and girls should never be treated differently as far as love and attention are concerned, there is a distinct difference when it comes to changing their diapers.

That's because boys have an apparatus that is not unlike a water cannon or, considering the oscillation, an in-ground sprinkler system. After the first two changes, for which I should have worn a raincoat and a pair of goggles, I was convinced that Xavier will grow up to be a firefighter.

It was a geyser on a geezer.

But I didn't mind at all. Eventually I learned to put a towel over the aforementioned anatomical feature while attending to the number two concern.

After one changing, Katie said to me, "Put Xavier's pants on."

I replied, "I don't think they'll fit me."

Xavier, I swear to God, smiled.

"Did Poppie make a joke?" Katie asked Xavier.

He smiled again. Then he burped. That's my boy!

Sue also pitched in, of course. She took some of the feedings, but mainly she prepared meals, something I couldn't do without having to call 911. Our main job, aside from enjoying our grandson, was to give some relief to Katie and Dave, who are wonderful parents, just like Lauren and Guillaume.

The day we left, I asked Katie, "How did I do? Was Lauren right?"

"You were good," Katie said. "You were really good. In fact, you were fantastic. Forget a nanny. You could be a manny. I'd hire you. If you ever retire," she added, "give me a call."

"Boys Will Be Boys"

As a guy who for almost forty years has been pretty much the lone source of testosterone in my immediate family (which has included one wife, two daughters, two granddaughters, two dogs, three out of four cats, and countless goldfish), I was thrilled to meet Xavier, with whom I plan to form a bond based on such important masculine benchmarks as whoopee cushions and the Three Stooges.

For expert advice in the fine art of corrupting male children and appalling the women who love them, I spoke with my buddy Tim Lovelette, who has two sons and six grandchildren, the last two, both born in the past year, boys.

"First off," Tim said, "you have to buy Xavier stuff you would never buy for your granddaughters."

That means, he added, shopping with the Johnson Smith Company, whose catalog features such timeless products as joy buzzers, squirting flowers, plastic teeth, remote-controlled tarantulas, X-ray glasses, and, of course, whoopee cushions.

"Where else are you going to get fake dog vomit?" Tim noted. "Or a carbide cannon? Did you ever see one of those things? They're awesome.

They shoot water and make a really loud noise. Women aren't going to buy this stuff for them. It's up to us. We have to keep the guy thing going."

That includes introducing boys to the Three Stooges.

"It's our solemn responsibility," Tim said. "Men love the Stooges and women hate them. It's a law of nature. Listen," he continued, "this is not about your grandson. It's about your relationship with him. You have to exercise your lack of maturity. All these women have matured over time. We haven't. And we can't let it happen to our grandsons."

What about Tim's sons, Marshall and Brendan?

"They had a very odd upbringing," Tim said. "That's because I'm their father. But I taught them all this stuff."

And now he's ready to teach it to his grandsons, Marshall III and Emmett, whose middle name is Timothy.

"There's something wrong with anyone who would name a kid after me," Tim said, adding that his wife, Jane, and their daughter, Amy, are never surprised by anything he does.

"They're waiting for this stuff to happen," Tim said.

But his daughter-in-law Sara, who is married to Marshall, and his son-in-law, Mel, who is married to Amy, the parents of Tim's grandkids, sometimes are surprised. So is Brendan's wife, Christie.

"I'll tell them, 'What, you didn't expect this? You knew what you had on your hands when you married into the family.' They still don't believe it," Tim said with no small amount of pride.

I said that Sue, Katie, and Lauren have come to expect stupidity from me. But even though Dave and Guillaume are also conditioned to it, they're occasionally taken aback by things I say or do.

"You'd think they would be used to it by now," said Tim, whose granddaughters are Anna, Camille, Colette, and Lydia. Mine are Chloe and Lilly.

But it's Marshall III, Emmett, and Xavier we want to get under our influence.

"You have to take Xavier out to lunch and order grilled octopus," Tim told me. "Or take him out for a cup of coffee. When you come back, tell the women the two of you had cigars. See how they react.

You can't do this stuff with girls. The women in my family are trying to condition my grandsons before they're released into my custody. But I have every intention of corrupting them."

And when the boys are older, said Tim, they can repay us.

"By the time Xavier is eight years old, he's your technical department," Tim said. "Buy a TV and he'll set it up. And you don't have to pay him. You can save the money for beer. He'll be too young to drink it anyway."

For now, however, it's vital that the seeds of masculine immaturity are planted.

"The whole war effort depends on you," Tim said. "And if you run out of stupid ideas, call me."

"Poppie's Back Story"

A little while back, I had a bad back. It was one of the few times that otherwise helpful people didn't say to me, "I have your back." And no wonder. Who'd want it?

The garbageman didn't. I threw my back out, but he wouldn't take it.

In fact, that's how I got a bad back. The garbageman had just taken away everything in the garbage bin, which was light and empty, just like my head. I was bringing the bin back to the backyard, which is not a bad backyard because I don't have to take care of it, though if I did, the backyard would no doubt give me a bad back.

But back to my story. I was carrying the bin back when I felt a sudden pain in my back. It was as if somebody (the garbageman, perhaps) had jammed a hot fireplace poker into it.

That wasn't the case, of course, because I don't have a fireplace and I don't play poker.

Still, as I limped painfully back to the house, it brought me back to the two other times I have had a bad back.

The first time was when I was carrying an air conditioner down a flight of stairs. That I wrenched my back was understandable because the typical air conditioner weighs about as much as a baby grand piano. Or, if you are not musically inclined, a dead body, which might as well have been mine.

The second time was not so understandable because I was bending down to get dishwashing liquid under the kitchen sink when a bolt of lightning coursed down my spine, preventing me from straightening up and making me the human equivalent of an isosceles triangle, an unfortunate comparison since I flunked high school geometry.

Every time I have had a bad back, I have talked with people who either have had a bad back themselves or have known other people who have had a bad back and have contradictory suggestions for treating it.

They are: exercise, relaxation, cold and/or heat. My favorite suggestion was to let somebody walk on my back. Unfortunately, I don't know Heidi Klum and would probably get stuck with Chris Christie.

Until this most recent flare-up, I thought the two best things for a bad back were rest and beer. But now I have an even better answer: grandchildren.

Recently, Chloe, four, and Lilly, seven months, spent the weekend with me and Sue, who has a great back. Frequently, however, she has a pain in the area directly south of it, a condition she attributes to yours truly. Only wine can help.

This time, Chloe and Lilly helped me. When they arrived, Chloe wanted me to pick her up so she could give me a kiss. She weighs thirty-six pounds, not an extraordinary amount for someone who has built up his muscles by doing twelve-ounce curls. But when that weight is moving in all directions while being held in your arms, it adds several long tons of pressure to an already sore back.

Miraculously, I didn't collapse. Chloe kissed me and said, "I love you, Poppie!" Suddenly, I felt a lot better.

Then I picked up Lilly, who weighs fourteen pounds, and kissed her. She cooed. I carried her around the house for a while, which helped me work the knots (sheepshank, not sailor's) out of my back.

For the next two days, I bent down to play with Lilly while she was in her bouncy seat, played hide-and-seek with Chloe, held Lilly to give her a bottle, lifted Chloe onto my lap so I could read to her, sprawled on the floor during tummy time with Lilly, and otherwise had a ball with the girls.

By the end of the weekend, I was cured. To stay that way, I will soon see my two-month-old, twelve-pound grandson, Xavier, whom I will carry around to keep in shape.

When it comes to feeling good, my grandkids have my back.

"The Graduate"

I have never been to a graduation at Yale, Harvard, or any other Ivy League school, mainly because I couldn't get into one of those prestigious institutions unless I broke in at night, in which case I would be arrested and sentenced to serve time in another kind of institution.

But I did attend a graduation at Old Steeple, a preschool in Aquebogue, New York, and its moving-up ceremony beat anything a university could put on. I admit to being prejudiced because Chloe was in the Class of 2017 and, I can proudly say, graduated magna cum little.

The impressive event began as Chloe and her classmates filed into the church above their school and waited for the formal procession past dozens of guests. They included Sue and yours truly, as well as Lauren, Guillaume, and Lilly, who is nine months old and won't be in preschool for another two years.

Mrs. Kramer, the teacher, and Mrs. Link, her assistant, guided the nineteen members of the graduating class into position. That's when Chloe spotted Sue and me sitting in the second row. Because she didn't expect us to be there, her eyes widened and she broke the line, rushing up to the first row and squealing, "Hi, Nini and Poppie!"

Sue and I smiled and waved.

Chloe looked at me and said, "I'm so glad you could make it, Poppie!" Then she said, "Doh!"

It's an utterance most recently made famous by Homer Simpson, but it was originated in the early 1930s by James Finlayson, eternal antagonist of Laurel and Hardy. Chloe and I have been saying it to each other since she learned to talk, so I returned the greeting.

Sue nudged me and whispered, "Stop fooling around."

Then we both indicated to Chloe that she should get back in line.

"OK, Nini and Poppie!" she chirped and, accompanied by Mrs. Kramer, reclaimed her spot.

The exchange drew an appreciative chuckle from the audience.

As "Pomp and Circumstance" did not play, the students walked up to the altar and took their seats on folding chairs that were arranged in a horseshoe shape. Mrs. Kramer stood at the microphone and welcomed the guests.

What she didn't do was give a commencement address, a refreshing switch from the typical graduation ceremony in which some bloviating speaker tells the graduates they are "the future of this great nation" and urges them to "go out and change the world," which would have been an unreasonable exhortation to kids whose idea of change not too long ago involved their diapers.

One by one, the students went up to the microphone and said a rehearsed line that introduced the next part of the program. Some were tentative.

Not Chloe. When it was her turn, she strode up to the mic and said in a strong voice, "We will now sing 'The More We Get Together'!" For emphasis, she elongated the last syllable, which drew a laugh and a round of applause from the audience.

Then the graduates sang the catchy song:

"The more we get together, the happier we'll be. Your friends are my friends, my friends are your friends. The more we get together, the happier we'll be."

When the hearty applause stopped, Chloe looked down in my direction and again said, "Doh!"

The crowd chuckled once more.

The rest of the program was just as delightful. At its conclusion, Mrs. Kramer stepped back up to the microphone to hand out diplomas. The first student she called was Chloe, who took the sheepskin and, with a flourish, bowed to the crowd, which responded with enthusiasm.

"She's tops in her class," I said to Sue, Lauren, Guillaume, and Lilly, who recently learned to clap and was doing so, perhaps unwittingly, for her big sister.

Afterward, everyone went downstairs to the school for milk and cookies. It was a fitting end to the best graduation I have ever attended.

Yale or Harvard couldn't have done better.

"Moe, Larry, and Poppie"

There are many reasons for a man to be proud of his grandchildren, as I am of my three, who are beautiful, smart, loving, and, even though the eldest is only four years old, more mature than their grandfather.

Now I can add one more reason: Xavier, at the tender age of four months, is a Three Stooges fan.

I made this delightful discovery when Sue and I took another road trip to visit the little guy.

The moment of revelation occurred on a sunny morning in Katie and Dave's bedroom, where I was watching Xavier while everyone else got ready for a day of fun, frolic, and, of course, infantile behavior. And I'm not talking about Xavier.

Anyway, I was upstairs with him, cooing and babbling (so was he), when Dave entered the room and said, "Having some guy time?"

"We sure are," I answered.

As Dave left to go back downstairs, he said, "If I hear any Three Stooges noises, I'm rushing right back up."

Answering the challenge, I did my award-winning Curly imitation, snapping my fingers and making funny faces as I exclaimed, "Nyuk, nyuk, nyuk!" and "Woo, woo, woo!"

Xavier smiled and started to wave his arms and kick excitedly.

I told him that many years ago I was first runner-up in the National Curly Howard Sound-Alike Contest (I won a hundred dollars and some Stooge paraphernalia in the telephone competition, whose winner was never identified and must have been an inmate somewhere).

I also told him that I once attended a Three Stooges convention in Pennsylvania and again was first runner-up, this time in the Curly Shuffle Contest, which was won by a four-year-old girl.

Xavier furrowed his brow as if to say, "Poor Poppie. What a knucklehead!"

Then I imitated my favorite Stooge, Shemp. I inhaled deeply and made the famous Shemp sound: "Ee-bee-bee-bee!"

Xavier — this is absolutely true — laughed out loud. I did it again. He giggled uncontrollably.

"I am so proud of him!" I said to Dave when he rushed back upstairs. "Xavier loves Shemp!"

Dave, a wonderful young man with a terrific sense of humor, kindly refrained from poking his father-in-law in the eyes.

"The surest sign of maturity in a man, if indeed it ever happens, is when he comes to appreciate Shemp," I told Dave. "Xavier is starting at a young age."

Just as the late, great original Stooge has a new fan, so does the new fan.

"Xavier is my little man," said Junior Bush, who lives across the street and is known as the mayor of the neighborhood.

Junior, seventy-three, a retired revenue collector, doesn't have kids of his own, but he does have ten nieces and nephews who look up to him as a father figure. Everyone on the block loves him.

I found out why when Junior knocked on Katie and Dave's door to warn me that my car would get ticketed and towed if I didn't move it for the street sweeper.

"I'll give you my parking space," Junior said.

I found the lone remaining spot across the street, so I didn't have to take up Junior on his nice offer, but I appreciated it.

"I love Katie and Dave," Junior told me. "And Xavier is just the cutest."

"I've been teaching him about the Three Stooges," I said.

Junior chuckled and replied, "You have to start them early."

Despite Dave's fears, I have. Every time I did my Shemp imitation, Xavier laughed. At least a dozen times over the next few days, whether he was in his car seat, on the changing table, or in my arms, when I said, "Ee-bee-bee-bee," he let out a baby guffaw.

The next time we get together, I am going to introduce Xavier to Moe, Larry, Curly, Shemp, and the other Stooges on video. Will he love them even more?

In the immortal words of Poppie doing his Curly imitation, "Soitenly! Nyuk, nyuk, yuk!"

"The Zezimas' Christmas Letter"

Since I am in the holiday spirit (and, having just consumed a mug of hot toddy, a glass of eggnog, and a nip of cheer, the holiday spirits are in me), I have once again decided to follow in that great tradition of boring everyone silly by writing a Christmas letter.

That is why I am pleased as punch (which I also drank) to present the following chronicle of the Zezima family, which includes Jerry, the patriarch; Sue, the matriarch; Katie and Lauren, the daughtersiarch; Dave and Guillaume, the sons-in-lawiarch; and Chloe, Lilly, and Xavier, the grandchildreniarch.

Dear friends:

It sure has been an exciting year for the Zezimas!

The year got off to a rocky start when Jerry had a kidney stone. He is sorry to have to number them like the Super Bowl, but it was Kidney Stone VI. Mercifully, this, too, did pass.

Also on the medical front, Jerry took a CPR class in which the instructor used him as a dummy. The other class members couldn't tell the difference.

To keep in good physical condition, Jerry won a one-day gym membership. He didn't exercise very strenuously, proving to be the biggest dumbbell there, but afterward he went to an adjacent bar and did twelve-ounce curls.

Continuing to show his commitment to a healthy lifestyle, Jerry attended a Wine Stomp Party at a vineyard and, re-creating a famous

"I Love Lucy" episode, climbed into a vat of grapes and stomped them with his bare feet. To ensure the health of the vineyard's customers, the grapes were thrown away.

Jerry may not have made his own wine, but he and Chloe did make their own ice cream. They went to a shop where the owner, impressed by Chloe's natural ability to pour in the ingredients but not by Jerry's pathetic incompetence at measuring them, allowed the dynamic duo to make a batch of honey-cinnamon. It was delicious, prompting the owner to tell Chloe, "Now you can say you taught your grandfather how to make ice cream."

Jerry, Sue, and Lauren took Chloe and Lilly on their first visit to the zoo, where humans were the wildest creatures and Jerry, an acknowledged oldster, was carded by a flirtatious young woman while buying beer for the adults in the group. He roared louder than the lions.

One of the proudest moments of the year occurred when Chloe graduated, magna cum little, from preschool. She had a prominent role in the ceremony, which was attended by Jerry, Sue, Lauren, Guillaume, and Lilly, and was tops in her class. Afterward, everyone had milk and cookies. Yale or Harvard couldn't have done better.

A milestone was reached when Lilly celebrated her first birthday. Big sister Chloe, who's four, helped her blow out the candle on her cupcake and, as their little friends applauded, helped her eat the cupcake, too. Talk about sisterly love!

And there was an addition to the family: Xavier, Katie and Dave's beautiful boy, made his grand entrance into the world. Sue and Jerry, aka Nini and Poppie, went on a road trip to meet him and Jerry quickly learned that changing diapers on a boy is a lot different from changing them on a girl. That's because boys have an apparatus that is not unlike a water cannon or, considering the oscillation, an in-ground sprinkler system. It was a geyser on a geezer.

But Jerry didn't mind because he got to do some male bonding. On a subsequent visit, Jerry introduced Xavier to the Three Stooges, making him giggle uncontrollably by doing Shemp imitations. The women, naturally, were thrilled.

Jerry Zezima

Xavier met cousins Chloe and Lilly on a visit to Nini and Poppie's house. The three adorable children had a ball, laughing, playing, and, not surprisingly, proving to be more mature than Poppie.

We hope your year has been fun-filled, too.

Merry Christmas with love and laughter from the Zezimas.

7

"The Good Guys"

"Mr. Sunshine"

Of our planet's many great meteorological mysteries — including why, since I am full of hot air, no hurricane in the past thirty years has been named after me — this one is the most baffling of all: What the hell is the difference between partly sunny and partly cloudy?

I never knew the answer because, with my limited comprehension of weather patterns, I get very few brainstorms. As I have sadly come to realize, it's not the heat, it's the stupidity.

But I now have a much clearer understanding of weather forecasting, which explains why it rains every time I wash my car, thanks to my favorite TV meteorologist, Lonnie Quinn.

I visited Lonnie, the lead weather anchor for WCBS-TV, at the CBS Broadcast Center in New York, the City That Never Sleets.

I had watched Lonnie's forecast the night before and, based on his prediction of a shower, which I took before I left the house, brought an umbrella. As usual, Lonnie was spot-on, mainly because the showers were spotty.

"Most people think I'm all wet, even during droughts," I told him, "but today you helped me avoid being a real drip."

"That's my job," said Lonnie, who has a sunny disposition, even on rainy days.

Since he's famous for rolling up his sleeves, I asked him if I could roll up mine, too.

"Go for it, big boy!" said Lonnie, who believes in the right to bare forearms.

On a roll, he said he was born and raised in Cheshire, Connecticut, about fifty miles from my hometown of Stamford.

"My brother Jeff was born in our house on January 11," said Lonnie, who's fifty-four.

"That's my birthday!" I said. "The only other person I know of who was born on that date was Alexander Hamilton, which means I will either have a hit Broadway show or be killed in a duel."

"You deserve a show," said Lonnie.

"Not as much as I deserve to be shot," I replied.

Too nice to argue the point, Lonnie said Jeff was born during a blizzard.

"Me, too," I said. "I've been perpetrating snow jobs ever since."

"But this storm was so bad that my mother couldn't get out to go to the hospital," Lonnie said. "My father delivered the baby upstairs and tied off the umbilical cord with a shoelace. Not long afterward, a cop arrived on a snowmobile. The next day, there was a story in the local paper. The headline said, 'Hero cop delivers baby.' That was the family's first big weather event."

"So how come your brother isn't a meteorologist?" I asked.

"He's smart," Lonnie answered. "He went into finance."

Lonnie, a multiple Emmy Award winner and a former soap opera actor, said his mother is smart, too, but she doesn't always watch his weather forecasts.

"I'll say, 'Mom, did you see me on TV last night?' and she'll say, 'Oh, honey, the news is so depressing, so I didn't watch.' Of course," Lonnie said, "I know she watches regularly. And I know she's proud of me."

So is his five-year-old daughter, Lily, one of his three children, the others being son Nate, twenty, and younger daughter Savy, three.

Lonnie's wife, Sharon, is director of international communications for the National Basketball Association.

Said Lonnie: "When I take Lily out for ice cream, she'll say to the person behind the counter, 'My daddy is a weatherman.' When the person says, 'That's nice,' Lily will say, 'He's on TV!' And when the person asks what channel, Lily will say, 'I don't know.' But I know she's proud of me, too."

And I was proud of Lonnie for educating me on meteorological terms such as "partly sunny" and "partly cloudy."

"What do you think the difference is?" Lonnie asked.

I thought for a moment and said, "The spelling."

"I didn't see that one coming!" Lonnie exclaimed as he gave me a high five. Then he said, "When it's partly cloudy, only part of the sky has clouds and there is more sun. And when it's partly sunny, only part of the sky has sun and there are more clouds."

"I often have my head in the clouds," I admitted, "but now you have cleared them up for me."

"Glad I could let a little sunshine in," Lonnie said with a bright smile.

"When it comes to TV meteorologists," I told him, "you rain supreme."

"Duke of Oil"

It's not every day that you get the oil changed in your car (in fact, it's every three thousand miles) and drive away feeling like you've just struck oil.

But that's the way I felt when I spoke with Tony Didio, a service adviser at Hyundai 112 in Medford, New York, where my car routinely goes for oil changes, filter replacements, and medical procedures such as open-hood surgery.

Tony is a car doctor who has prescriptions not only for a healthy vehicle ("If you can't stop, those are the brakes"), but for a healthy lifestyle ("Never stand in front of a shooter at an archery range").

Tony also is an archer who has a point.

"I'm right on target," he told me.

"That pun made me quiver," I responded. "Do you know what Custer wore at Little Bighorn?"

"What?" Tony said.

"An Arrow shirt," I answered.

Since I don't have a Pierce-Arrow, which stopped manufacturing automobiles a decade and a half before I was born, I asked Tony about my 2014 Hyundai Santa Fe.

"When you change the oil in my car," I wondered, "do you use extra-virgin olive oil?"

"No," Tony said. "I'd use that on pizza. But we don't serve it here."

Ironically, Tony began his automotive career at his father's pizzeria in Plainview, New York.

"I was twelve when I started working there," said Tony, who's now sixty-five. "But I was always interested in cars. I used to clean off the ones that came over on boats from Germany, so I switched from olive oil to motor oil."

In 1971, Tony officially entered the car business when he went to work for a guy who was a mechanic for legendary race-car driver and designer Briggs Cunningham.

"Did you ever want to race in the Indy 500?" I asked.

"No," said Tony. "But I'd have a better chance there than I would here. New York drivers are crazy."

"You're a New York driver," I pointed out.

"Yes," Tony acknowledged. "But I'm not crazy enough to ruin my car. Then I'd have to fix it."

He's had to fix plenty of other people's cars in his forty-five years in the business, during which he has learned that women know just as much about cars as men do. And they're not as cheap.

"Like the guy whose brakes were worn down to the rotors, metal to metal, so I changed them," Tony recalled. "The guy got all bent out of shape, just like his brakes, and insisted I put the old ones back in because he didn't want to pay for new ones. Then he drove off. I was waiting for him to come back with a smashed front end because he couldn't stop. I should have put him up on a lift and examined his head."

Tony hasn't repaired cars since he slipped on a patch of ice while carrying an engine and threw his back out.

"I threw it out, but nobody would take it," Tony said with a deadpan expression, which he admitted is better than an oil-pan expression. "You have to have a sense of humor in this business," he noted.

Tony, who loves to joke around with his customers, recalled the time a woman heard a ticking sound in her car and thought her husband had planted a bomb in it.

"I guess they weren't getting along," Tony said perceptively. "So I told her I was going to call 911. I kept her in suspense for about ten minutes. Then I said, 'I'm only kidding. There's no bomb in the car.' She was greatly relieved."

Tony said people are always telling him that he should be a stand-up comic.

"I can't stand up that long," he said. "My feet get tired."

But not too tired for this husband, father, and soon-to-be grandfather to stand in the kitchen occasionally and, recalling the pizza days of his youth, make a delicious Italian dinner.

When I told Tony I'm not handy enough to be either a mechanic or a cook, he gave me the secret of his success: "If you just remember that motor oil goes in cars and olive oil goes on pizza, you'll be OK."

"You Have to Hand It to Him"

Whenever Sue asks me to tidy up the bathroom, I feel like throwing in the towel because I could never get it to look as nice as the porcelain convenience at a place like the Waldorf Astoria.

So imagine my surprise and delight when I met a guy whose job is to throw in the towel in the porcelain convenience at the Waldorf Astoria.

I attended a dinner at the famed New York City hotel, which is ritzy enough to rival the Ritz but does not, to my knowledge, serve Ritz crackers, at least not in the bathroom, where I went to answer the call of nature, which called collect.

As I was washing up (according to some people, I have been washed up for years), I was handed a towel by a gentleman dressed to the tens, which is even better than the nines. He was nattily attired (if we were in the ladies' room, he would have been Natalie Attired) in a white, pleated, wing-collar shirt; a black, crisply tied bow tie; a neat black vest; sharply creased black pants, and shiny black shoes.

I, dressed to the sevens in a wrinkled gray suit, took the perfectly folded paper towel, which was embossed with the Waldorf logo, and dried my hands, though not before dripping water all over my dull black shoes.

"Would you like another towel, sir?" washroom attendant Alex Giannikouris asked politely.

"Thank you," I replied as he handed me one. "Now I can shine my shoes."

I also took a shine to Alex, who has worked at the Waldorf for thirty-two years and, judging from the many visitors who stopped in to get tidied up themselves, is even more popular than the celebrities who frequent the premises.

"Alex!" exclaimed one gentleman (we were, after all, in a room marked "Gentlemen," which made me wonder what I was doing there). "Como esta?"

"Muy bien," responded Alex, a native of Greece who speaks about half a dozen languages.

The two men carried on a brief conversation in Spanish, at the end of which Alex said, "Adios!"

Another man, tall, handsome, and bedecked in a tuxedo, greeted Alex with a handshake — after, of course, drying his hands on the towel Alex gave to him.

"Are you a regular?" I asked the visitor.

"What?" he replied indignantly.

"A regular," I explained. "Not irregular."

"Yes," said the man, who seemed relieved. "I've known Alex for years. He's a great guy."

That was the consensus among the other visitors, one of whom spoke with Alex in French and another in Greek.

"I even know a little Korean," Alex said, in perfect English.

Then he regaled me with stories of the celebrities who have stopped in to admire themselves in the mirror.

"The best," Alex said, "was Frank Sinatra."

"Did he do it his way?" I asked.

Alex smiled and said, "Yes. He was very nice and very generous. A big tipper."

"How much money did he give you?" I wondered.

"I can't say," Alex replied. "The IRS might find out."

At least Alex won't get in trouble with the Social Security Administration. That's because Bill Clinton, when he was president, signed Alex's Social Security card. Alex pulled it out of his wallet and showed me the inscription: "To Alex: Thanks, Bill Clinton."

"Did you vote for him?" I asked.

"I don't talk politics in here," said Alex, who was happy to talk about George Burns ("a funny guy"), Al Pacino ("he washed his face in the sink"), and Ingrid Bergman.

"Ingrid Bergman was in the men's room?" I spluttered.

"No," said Alex. "I saw her upstairs. She was very beautiful. One other time, I saw Pope John Paul II upstairs. As he walked past, he gave me a blessing."

But Alex said he feels especially blessed to be married to Maria, his wife of thirty-nine years.

"One woman for all that time? Why not?" Alex said with a broad smile.

"Do you show your appreciation by tidying up the bathroom at home?" I wondered.

"No, she does it," admitted Alex, who leaves the tidying up at the Waldorf to a cleaning crew.

He and Maria have three grown children and two young grandchildren.

"I'm a grandpa, too," I said. "I'm called Poppie."

"I'm called Papou, which is Greek for grandfather," said Alex, who is sixty-three and plans to retire soon.

"I've had a good career at the Waldorf," he said. "I've met a lot of nice people. But one of these days it will be time to go. And then," he added, "I'll really throw in the towel."

"He's a Hot Ticket"

If I ever won Powerball, I'd never collect the money because I would either put the ticket somewhere in the house for safekeeping and never find it again or realize I had the winning numbers and drop dead from shock.

But that hasn't stopped me from playing when the stakes get high enough (the most I ever won was two bucks, which I used to buy another ticket) because it gives me an excuse to go to my favorite store, 50 Percent Off Cards in Coram, New York.

On a morning when the jackpot was one hundred and fifty-five million dollars, I walked up to the counter and handed two dollars to owner Peter Shah, who handed me a ticket and said, "You are going to win. I know it."

"If I do," I replied, "I'll share the money with you."

"If you don't," he said with a smile, "I'll find you."

Peter, fifty, who immigrated to the United States from India in 1993, doesn't need the money. That's because, in the estimation of his customers, including me, he's priceless.

"Peter is wonderful," said Ann, who came in to buy a ticket for herself and four of her co-workers, adding: "We recently won five hundred dollars, so I think he's a good-luck charm, too."

"Then how come I haven't won that kind of money?" wondered Peter, who said he buys a ticket once in a while but that, like me, the most he has ever won is two bucks. "A couple of years ago, somebody won a million dollars here," Peter recalled. "I don't know who it was."

"You didn't find the guy like you said you were going to find me?" I asked.

"Maybe he dropped dead," Peter theorized.

Bobby Jolly described Peter as "a great guy, a beautiful man" as he paid for the Daily Racing Form. "I don't play the lottery," Bobby said. "I play the horses. I've been following them for years."

"You must run really fast," I suggested.

"I should enter the Belmont Stakes," Bobby said. "Then people could bet on me."

Suzanne, who recently won four dollars in her office pool, said Peter is the store's main attraction.

"This gentleman is very kind," she said. "And he knows what I play. What do I play, Peter?"

"Mega Millions," he reminded her. "One day, you'll win the mega part of it."

"That would be nice," Suzanne said. "The most I've ever won is seven dollars. I can't quit my job with that."

As Suzanne left, in walked Malcolm Abrams, eighty-six, a retired statistician who is Peter's most loyal customer and half of a comedy team that performs daily routines for amused patrons.

"If I knew I was going to be interviewed," Malcolm told me, "I would have worn clean underwear."

"How would you describe Peter?" I asked.

"He's a great guy," Malcolm said. "That's what he would say if you interviewed him."

"I would say that if I was sleeping," Peter retorted.

"I don't play the numbers. I tell Peter I print my own money," said Malcolm, who volunteers at a nearby hospital.

"He doesn't wash his hands when he operates on people," Peter said.

"I do brain surgery," Malcolm said. "And I've been carrying the weight of Peter all these years."

"When were you born?" Peter asked Malcolm. "It was 1878, right?"

"I'm not that old," Malcolm shot back. "It was 1879. Let's get it straight."

"I gave Jerry your Social Security number," Peter told Malcolm.

"See what I have to put up with?" Malcolm said to me as he paid Peter for a newspaper. "I come in here every day because I feel I have a spiritual obligation to Peter. He wouldn't survive without me."

With that, Malcolm, who lives around the corner but has resided in many places, including thirty-one years in Schenectady ("It took me that long to learn how to spell it," he said), tipped his cap and said to Peter, "If you're lucky, you'll see me tomorrow."

I was lucky to have witnessed all of that but not so fortunate with my Powerball ticket: I didn't get even one number.

"One of these days you'll win," Peter said a couple of days later. "And you won't drop dead. Then," he added with a smile, "you can share the money with me."

8

"We Can Work It Out"

"Don't Quit Your Day Job"

When my kids were young and had already fallen into the expensive habit of eating every day, I came to a sad realization: If people waited until they could afford to have children, the human race would die out.

Now that my kids are grown and have kids of their own, which means I don't have to feed them anymore, I have come to another sad realization: If people waited until they could afford to retire, most of them would die at their desks.

This, I fear, is the fate that awaits me. My bosses would argue that nobody could tell the difference because I'd be just as effective as I am now. At least they wouldn't have to pay me anymore.

Still, to get an idea of how long I could survive once I quit my job, or if I'd have to continue working until my kids retired, at which point they could feed me every day, I met with Jeff Sena, a regional consultant with Fidelity Investments, a multinational financial services corporation that is based in Boston and does business with the company that, in its limited wisdom, employs me.

"How old are you?" Jeff asked me at the start of the hourlong session.

"Old enough to know better," I replied.

"Do you?" he wondered.

"No," I said.

"Then I need to know your age," he said, "because Social Security won't accept 'old enough to know better' on your paperwork."

"OK," I conceded, "I'm sixty-three."

"You don't look it," Jeff said. "And you don't act it."

"I'm shockingly immature," I responded. "It makes me seem younger."

"I wouldn't put that on your paperwork, either, or you'd have to work even longer," said Jeff, who is sixty-five but doesn't look or act it himself.

"You're sixty-five and you're not retired?" I said incredulously. "Can't you afford it?"

"I can, but I love what I do," said Jeff, who also loves hiking and belongs to the Appalachian Mountain Club.

"You must have clients from all walks of life," I noted, adding: "People are always telling me to take a hike."

"You should," Jeff said with a smile. "But don't take one now because we have to go over your finances."

"That shouldn't take long," I said, producing the required documents, including bank statements, income information, and investment records. "As you can see, I haven't won Powerball."

"Neither have I," said Jeff, who scanned the figures and told me that I have a good RPM.

"My car has a good RPM, too," I said. "And it will retire before I do."

"I'm talking about your Retirement Preparedness Measurement," Jeff said. "But more important than that is your FRA."

"My car doesn't have one of those," I said.

"No," countered Jeff, "but you do. It stands for Full Retirement Age."

The standard FRA, Jeff said, is sixty-six, though people can draw on Social Security beginning at age sixty-two.

"I can't draw on anything except my grandchildren's coloring books," I said.

"If you were retired, you'd have plenty of time for that," Jeff said. "But you'd be better off working until you were seventy because Social Security payments go up eight percent a year until that age."

Jeff said he could plan a retirement strategy for me until I am ninety-four and Sue until she is ninety-six. "Women live longer than men," he noted.

"If it weren't for my wife," I said, "I would have been dead long ago."

Nonetheless, I told Jeff, longevity runs in the family.

"You must have good genes," he said.

"Of course," I responded. "My wife does all of my clothes shopping."

"The question is," Jeff said at the end of the session, "would your wife want you around all the time if you were both retired?"

"I'd probably drive her crazy," I said.

"Then you should keep working," Jeff suggested. "You can drive your bosses crazy instead."

"Nice Work If You Can Get It"

Whenever I attempt to do something I can't do — sing, dance, perform surgery — somebody tells me not to quit my day job. The only people who want me to quit are my bosses, who don't realize that the reason I have my day job is that I am spectacularly unqualified to do anything else.

Still, you never know when you will no longer be gainfully (or, in my case, ungainfully) employed. So, because I have had a fair career, I went to a career fair. It was held, perhaps not coincidentally, at the company where I work.

The first thing I found out, after stopping at a table sponsored by my company, is that I couldn't get a job with my company. That's because they were looking for someone to provide technical support.

"Technically speaking, my grandchildren are more advanced than I am," I admitted, "which means they would have to support me."

"Can you do anything else?" asked Craig Brusseler, talent manager for operations.

"Aside from telling bad jokes, I have no talent," I said. "And hospital patients wouldn't trust me to do operations."

But Chrissy Huber, a sales recruiter, thought I had promise.

"You have a good personality," she noted, "so you could go door to door to convince people who have switched to another cable company to come back to us."

"What if somebody thought I was a scam artist and called the cops?" I wondered. "I don't want to go back to prison."

Chrissy raised her eyebrows, extended her hand, and said, "Good luck with your job search."

I had bad luck at the next table, which was sponsored by BMW.

"We are looking for technicians," said recruiter Stefan Schedel.

"I'd have an easier time transcribing the Dead Sea Scrolls than telling you what's going on under the hood of a car," I confessed.

"I'm afraid you're not the kind of person we're looking for," said Renai Ellison, another recruiter.

"Could I at least get a free car out of the deal?" I asked.

I didn't. But I did get a free tote bag. I dropped in the Frisbee and the pen I got from my company.

Next I stopped at the Liberty Mutual table, where Maureen Baranello and Robert Moore were looking for someone to sell insurance.

"It involves outside referrals," Maureen said.

"I don't like working outside," I replied. "What if it rains?"

"Buy a raincoat and an umbrella," Robert suggested.

I told the two recruiters about the time I got into a car accident that was caused by a guy whose GPS told him to go the wrong way down a one-way street.

"Your company covered the damage," I said.

"You can tell that story to potential customers," said Maureen.

"Does the job include crunching numbers?" I inquired.

"Yes," Robert said. "Lots of them."

"I'll have to disqualify myself," I said. "One of the reasons I went into journalism is because I can't do math. I'd bankrupt your company in a week."

I'd do the same to Bethpage Federal Credit Union, whose recruiter, Amanda Shatel, said I couldn't refinance my mortgage so I wouldn't have any more payments.

"I helped bail out the banks," I pointed out. "Would yours do the same for me?"

"Sorry," said Amanda, who gave me a free letter opener so I could open my mortgage statements.

I visited other tables — including those sponsored by Riverhead Building Supply, where I got a paint stick and a rubber hammer; The Arbors, which runs assisted living communities, where I got another pen; and David Lerner Associates, an investment broker, where I got a handshake — but nothing panned out.

"Did you go to the career fair?" one of my bosses asked when I returned to my desk.

"Yes," I said.

"How'd it go?" he wondered.

"Bad news," I said. "I'm not quitting my day job."

"The Call of the Riled"

If you were to call me on my old iPhone to ask when telephone technology reached its peak, I would have told you it was the day Alexander Graham Bell invented it and that the entire industry has been going downhill ever since, except you wouldn't hear me because the reception would be so bad that it would seem like the nearest cellphone tower was on Pluto, which would give Disney an excuse to charge me for phone service.

Now that I have a new iPhone, I would be happy to discuss telephone technology with you, unless I didn't recognize your number, thought you were a scam artist, and refused to pick up.

Still, I owe my technological upgrade to Josh Frankel, a retail sales consultant who knows more about phones than Bell himself, which admittedly isn't difficult considering the inventor died almost a hundred years ago and isn't on my list of contacts.

Speaking of which, the contacts mysteriously disappeared from my old phone, ascending into the iCloud on a day when it wasn't even iCloudy. It was the final insult from a device that had no doubt been the inspiration for an advertising campaign that asked the eternal telephonic question: "Can you hear me now?"

"Yes, I can," Josh said when Sue and I went to a nearby AT&T store to exchange our old phones for newer models that, in my case, wouldn't do much good anyway since nobody wants to talk with me.

My enthusiasm over the fact that Josh could actually hear me was tempered somewhat by the additional fact that I wasn't on the phone at the time.

"You're sitting right next to me," Josh pointed out. "If I couldn't hear you, a phone wouldn't do me much good, either."

I heard Josh when he politely told me that I had the stegosaurus of phones, the iPhone 4, which I bought in 2012 and hadn't really learned how to use aside from: (a) forgetting where I put it, (b) butt dialing complete strangers, and (c) punctuating almost every conversation with indelicate language when, because I was invariably in a dead zone, it seemed like I was talking to a mime.

"You have to move up," Josh said.

"You mean I'd get better reception on the roof?" I asked.

"No," Josh replied. "I mean you need a better phone."

Then he said that most people don't use the phone part of phones anymore.

"Wouldn't that be like not using the driving part of cars anymore?" I wondered.

"I guess so," Josh said. "But if someone calls me, I know it's not important. If it's important, they'll text me."

Josh, who's twenty-seven and has been working in the wireless industry for eight years, knows whereof he speaks, even if it's not into a phone. That's why he was so helpful to me and Sue, who had problems of her own because her phone, an iPhone 5S, lost all of her emails.

"Fortunately," Sue told Josh, "I have an iPad."

"Do you have an iPad?" Josh asked me.

"No," I responded. "But I do have iTeeth."

Nonetheless, we both needed new phones. Josh suggested the iPhone 8, which has a larger screen and more advanced features.

Josh transferred everything from our old phones to our new ones, though he couldn't recover my contacts, which numbered about a hundred and probably included people I had never heard of.

"You'll have to start all over," Josh said.

"That's OK," I told him. "One of the first people I am going to put on there is you. What's your number?"

Josh gave it to me, then showed me how to set up my contact list.

"Thanks," I said. "I'd ask my four-year-old granddaughter, who knows how to break into her mother's phone by circumventing the password, but she isn't here."

"Put her on your contact list, too," Josh suggested. "I'm sure she'd love to talk with you. And now that you have a new phone, you'll come through loud and clear."

"The Benefits of the Doubt"

When it comes to health care, the most important question facing the American people is this: Is the pain reliever you need to get rid of the headache caused by your employer's open enrollment covered under medical insurance or do you have to spend thousands of dollars in deductibles before you can write off a bottle of aspirin?

That's what I asked a very nice and very knowledgeable human resources coordinator named Luann, who helped me navigate the process because Chloe isn't on the payroll and is already covered under Guillaume's plan.

"My niece is better on the computer than I am, although I'm an online shopper, so I'm really good at this," said Luann, who had been on the job for only three weeks before the rollout.

"Too bad the company isn't rolling out the barrel," I said.

"That would help," Luann replied as we sat at a monitor in the HR department and she showed me how to log on to the program.

There were four categories: benefits, health, money, and protection.

"Is there a Powerball option?" I asked.

"I'm afraid not," Luann replied. "If there was, I wouldn't be here."

Then we hit the initials: HSA (health savings account), FSA (flexible spending account), and, the one that really stunned me, STD.

"Please tell me it doesn't stand for what I think it does," I spluttered.

"It stands for short-term disability," Luann assured me. "Why?" she added with a smile. "What did you think it stands for?"

"Something that I'm sure isn't covered," I said.

I was already signed up for the company's dental and vision plans, but for the past two years I have been on Sue's medical plan because it's less expensive.

"Her deductible isn't as high as ours," I explained. "But no matter what plan you're on, with deductibles these days, you pretty much have to be in a train wreck for them to take effect."

"There's a simple solution," Luann said. "Don't take the train."

"Good advice," I said. "But if something happened, I'd have to pay out of my own pocket. And my pocket isn't big enough to hold all that money."

"So what's the answer?" Luann asked.

I told her the absolutely true story of my three unsuccessful campaigns for vice president of the United States, in 1992, 1996, and 2000, when my running mate, media prankster Alan Abel, was the presidential candidate.

"He ran under the name of Porky," I told Luann. "I used my nickname, Zez. We were the Gershwin-inspired ticket of Porky and Zez. We ran under the banner of the Cocktail Party. We came up with our health-care plan in New York City, so we called it Big Apple Coverage. Since an apple a day keeps the doctor away, we proposed a ten-cent co-pay on every apple. That way, everyone could afford medical care."

"I would have voted for you," Luann said.

"Some people did," I told her. "They probably couldn't afford their prescription medications."

"So there still isn't an answer to the health-care problem," Luann said.

"Yes, there is," I responded. "Porky and I had another proposal: Everybody in America becomes a member of Congress. That way, we'd have the same plan they do and we're all covered. Either that or kick Congress off their plan and make them shop for insurance like the rest of us."

"It's too bad you didn't run again last time," Luann said.

"I'm old now, so if I ran, I'd sprain an ankle or blow out a knee," I said. "And I wouldn't meet the deductible."

I thanked Luann for her help and good humor but said I was going to stick with Sue's medical plan.

"Stay healthy," Luann said, though after dealing with me, she no doubt needed a pain reliever. I hope it's covered.

"Show Them the Money"

I have very little influence, even in my own home, and an endorsement from me is usually the kiss of death. But that has not stopped me from trying to get raises for other people, which is a pretty nice gesture considering I can't get one for myself.

My campaign to improve the professional lives of folks I barely know began when I noticed that the receipts I get at supermarkets, pharmacies, post offices, health centers, car dealerships, and other such places include surveys I am asked to fill out so I can let management know what I think of the service and if the employees who help me deserve commendations, promotions, or, ultimately, raises.

Whenever I go to a store to buy a toothbrush or a box of Twinkies, which is why I need the toothbrush, I am handed a receipt long enough to encircle the Green Bay Packers.

On this receipt are coupons for things I don't need, such as feminine hygiene products, and at the end is a survey I have to go online to fill out, a process that often takes longer than the shopping experience itself.

I wondered: Does putting in a good word for someone actually help?

"We do look at the surveys," said Fredy, a supervisor at the post office branch near my house. "Unfortunately, I can't give the employees raises. I can't even give myself a raise."

Jeffrey, who works behind the counter, said of Fredy, "He comes from a poor family. When they named him, they could only afford one D."

"Now you'll never get a raise," Fredy said.

"The first time I saw one of those long receipts," Jeffrey told me, "I thought, 'Another tree has fallen.' But if you want to fill out the survey, be my guest. Just watch out for paper cuts."

I went home, got online, and gave Jeffrey a glowing review. When I went back a week later, I asked him if it did any good.

"Well," he said, "I'm still here. I don't know whether to thank you or not."

At the pharmacy, Christina, the morning shift supervisor, said that even if she gets the highest marks on a survey, she can't get a raise.

"I'm capped," she explained.

"You're not wearing a cap," I pointed out. "And you deserve a raise."

"I do," Christina agreed. "Even my boss said so."

"Then what good are the surveys?" I asked.

Said Christina, "That's the sixty-four-thousand-dollar question."

"Sixty-four thousand bucks would be a nice raise," I said.

"It would put me in a higher tax bracket," Christina noted. "Not that I would complain."

"I'll see what I can do," I told her.

"Thanks," she said. "Just be sure to spell my name right. I don't want anybody else to get the money."

One person who definitely deserves a raise is Tony, the service adviser at the dealership where I take my car for service.

"Whatever you're getting paid, it's not enough," I told him.

"My boss would probably say that I'm lucky I get paid at all," Tony retorted.

"Nonsense," I said. "You're the best."

"I sure have you fooled," Tony said. "But go ahead and take the survey. If I still have a job, it'll be a miracle."

I gave Tony the highest marks, along with a gushing comment. The next day, I got an email from his boss, who assured me that Tony is still working there and agreed that he is, indeed, terrific. No word, however, on whether he'll get a raise.

Since then, I have filled out surveys for my dermatologist, the woman who helped me with a computer problem, and the guy who replaced my cracked windshield. All, I trust, remain employed.

One person I haven't put in a good word for is myself.

"If there were a survey for what you do," my boss said, "do you think you'd get a raise?"

"I'd probably end up owing you money," I said.

"Good," he said. "I could use a raise. Working with you, I deserve one."

"All Hands on Tech"

In a world of rapidly increasing technology, which I understand about as well as I do the theory of relativity, which states that my youngest relatives, who happen to be my grandchildren, know more about this stuff than I do, there is one question that stands out as the most vexing of all:

How many months of my life have I spent waiting for that little circle on my computer screen to stop spinning?

To get the answer to this and other confounding computer conundrums, I tapped two tech titans, Karen Woodward and Vinny

Demasi, who are among the nice, talented, and very helpful IT folks where I work.

"The little circle used to be an hourglass and you had to wait for it to fill up," Vinny said.

"That's why it seemed like an hour before I could do anything," I recalled.

"Now it's a spinning circle," Karen said. "If you look at it too long, you'll get dizzy."

"I'm that way already," I told her.

Karen, sixty-three, who has been in the computer field for nineteen years, and Vinny, thirty, who has been in the business for nine years, work on the Help Desk and have patiently and expertly helped me and countless colleagues with problems ranging from the simple, like signing in, to the complex, which involves rebooting.

"My definition of rebooting," I said, "is putting your foot through the screen."

"Then you'd have to pay for a new computer," Vinny pointed out.

"And," Karen added, "you'd probably break your foot."

When I said that computers run the world and that IT workers are the linchpins of our existence, Karen said, "I wish I had put that on my self-evaluation."

"Break into the system and add it," I suggested. "I'd do it for you, but I don't know your password. I can barely remember mine."

"That," Vinny said, "is one of the problems we deal with every day."

There are plenty of others, he continued, like when people call to say that their computer screens are upside down.

"Have you asked if the people are upside down?" I wondered.

"If that were the case," said Vinny, "I'd go over and take a picture."

"We get calls for everything," Karen said. "Your coffee maker doesn't work? Plug it in. But if your computer is on fire, we can't help you over the phone."

"We'd recommend a fire extinguisher," Vinny said.

"How about marshmallows?" I suggested.

"You could stick them on the end of a ruler," said Karen.

"Most of the time, it's not that extreme," Vinny noted. "The people we deal with are really nice — when they're not yelling at the computer — and we like helping them."

It's true, Vinny acknowledged, that older people such as yours truly aren't as computer savvy as younger ones.

"I have three young grandchildren and they're more technologically advanced than I am," I said.

"I have a one-year-old granddaughter," Karen said. "I was babysitting her the other day and my daughter texted me on my phone. All of a sudden I saw this little finger like a toothpick scrolling up. She already knows what to do."

"My one-year-old daughter knows how to go on YouTube," Vinny said. "On my phone, she skips ads in the bottom right corner. She pulls the bottom up to show related videos."

"Even I didn't know that," Karen admitted.

"I didn't teach her," said Vinny. "She saw me and my wife doing it. Kids are really smart these days."

"It's a good thing there are child labor laws or they'd be working in IT," I said.

"And take our jobs," said Vinny.

"Then," Karen told me, "you'd have to ask a toddler to show you how to get that little circle on your computer screen to stop spinning."

9

"Miscellaneous Musings"

"A Traffic Ticket Hits Home"

Today's Ridiculous Banking Question is: What's the faster way to lose your house, don't pay the mortgage or don't pay a traffic ticket?

If you don't know the answer, you are probably living in your car.

That's the lesson Sue and I learned during a home refinancing odyssey that took three attempts in as many years and was almost ruined by, of all things, a red-light camera.

The first attempt failed because my credit score was considered more important than my pulse, which before the housing bubble burst was pretty much all you needed to qualify for a loan.

The second attempt failed because Sue and I committed the unpardonable sin of actually paying both our mortgage and our line of credit on time each month. We would have been better off if we had fallen hopelessly behind and blown the money in Atlantic City.

Praying the third time would be the charm, I went back to the bank and spoke with Kim Delman, a senior mortgage loan officer who is so nice, so smart, and so good that she ought to run the Federal Reserve System.

Kim, who worked diligently with us in our first two attempts, was determined to see us succeed this time.

In trying to combine our mortgage, which was at another bank, and our line of credit, which was at Kim's bank, I went through the Process From Hell: countless phone calls in which I had to listen carefully because the menu options had changed (restaurants change their menu options less often than the average company); give the last four digits of my Social Security number and my date of birth, just to prove I'm a geezer; and come up with yet another seemingly irrelevant thing the underwriter wanted, which surprisingly did not include my high school transcript or my underwear receipts.

Then came the clincher: After we shelled out four hundred and fifty-five dollars for an appraisal, which valued our house at three hundred and fifteen thousand dollars, Kim informed us that we were in danger of being rejected yet again, this time for a three-year-old unpaid traffic ticket worth a grand total of seventy-five dollars.

"There's a lien on your house," Kim said.

"Nothing's leaning on my house," I replied. "Not even a ladder, because I'm afraid of heights."

"You have to get this cleared up," Kim warned, "or the bank won't let you close."

I was put in touch with Leticia Glenn-Jones, a very pleasant home services specialist ("a fancy title for processor," she explained), who said the underwriter did, indeed, want this black mark off my criminal record.

"Let me get this straight: Seventy-five dollars is worth more than three hundred and fifteen thousand dollars," I said. "Is this the new math?"

"I'm afraid so," Leticia said sympathetically.

It turned out that a red-light camera caught Sue going through, yes, a red light. She received a notice in the mail in 2013 but forgot about it until the underwriter kindly noted that if we didn't pay up, we couldn't close. Sue sent a check for seventy-five dollars, plus late fees, which brought the total to one hundred and five dollars and, at long last, allowed us to refinance.

"It happens more often than you think," Kim said afterward. "It's those red-light cameras. Since they were installed, there have been tons of cases like this."

In twenty-one years at the bank, she has seen just about everything.

"You and Sue may have set the record for the longest time it took to refinance," said Kim, adding that her most unusual customer was a guy who applied for a mortgage in 1995 and, under assets, listed a cow.

"He said it was worth five hundred dollars," Kim said.

"Was he trying to milk the bank for money?" I asked.

"I don't know," said Kim. "But believe it or not, he qualified."

"I guess he didn't have any traffic tickets," I said.

I thanked Kim for all her hard work and promised that Sue and I would keep up on our payments.

"From now on," I said, "we'll pay the mortgage online. After all, we don't want to drive to the bank and risk losing our house by getting another ticket."

"No Bed of Roses"

Early to bed and early to rise makes a man healthy, wealthy, and sore as hell, especially if he has to move not just one bed but two, after which he is convinced he will soon be on his deathbed.

Sue considers me a strange bedfellow, which is why it took both of us to drive up to Stamford, disassemble a bed, load it into a rental truck, drive it back down to our house on Long Island, unload it, deposit it in our living room, disassemble a bed in an upstairs bedroom, bring it downstairs, load it into my car, drive it to Lauren's house, go back home, bring the first bed upstairs, and reassemble it in the aforementioned bedroom. All of this involved headboards, footboards, box springs, and mattresses.

I'm exhausted just thinking about it.

And I didn't even mention that more furniture, including a kitchen table and a set of chairs, was involved.

Fortunately, it didn't happen all in one day. Also, we had help. And we are grateful to Sue's mother and sister for their generosity (and, in the case of Sue's sister, physical assistance) in giving us, respectively, the bed and the kitchen set.

Still, for someone my age (old enough to know better), it's hard work, which I have always tried to avoid.

This is the best time of life because you can still do everything you have always done, but if there's something you don't want to do, you can pull the age card.

"I don't think I should be lugging furniture anymore," you might say to no one in particular, because no one in particular will listen to you.

Sure enough, it fell on deaf ears. And those ears belong to Sue, who pretended not to hear my feeble excuses (hernia, heart attack, death) about why we could live without all the exertion.

I must say, however, that we are a good team: Sue's the brains, I'm the pawn. So we joined forces to get the job done.

The worst part of bedding against the odds involves: (a) mattresses and (b) stairs.

The mattress of one of the two beds has handles; the other doesn't. With the former, at least you have something to grab hold of; with the latter, you have to try to grasp the smooth edge and lift, pull, push, slip, slide, or, if you are not careful, drop it down an entire flight of stairs. Or vice-versa, though it's impossible to drop a mattress up a flight of stairs because it will only slide back down with you holding on, handles or no handles, until you both crash to the floor.

It's not that a mattress is heavy (any Olympic weightlifter can hoist one for at least three seconds before EMTs have to be called), but it's definitely unwieldy. That is why Sue and I had so much trouble navigating each of them, not just up and down stairs, but around corners, over railings, and past a wall full of family photos that include one of me when I was a baby (it was taken last week).

Then there are the headboards and the footboards, which are meant to be dropped on your head and your foot, respectively. These not only are unwieldy but are approximately as heavy as a full-grown rhinoceros, without the horn but with posts that can do just as much damage if they hit you in the wrong spot. After one such near-catastrophe, I was lucky I didn't have to go to Vienna, either for medical treatment or to join the Boys Choir.

Finally, Sue and I got the first bed upstairs and put it together, a herculean feat that called for several infusions of cold beer.

That night, we collapsed on our own bed. It was the best night's sleep we ever had.

"For Cold Times' Sake"

On January 11, 1954, a date which will live in infancy, I made my grand entrance into the world while a blizzard raged outside the maternity ward at Stamford Hospital. I have been perpetrating snow jobs ever since.

So you might think that I like winter. Actually, of the four seasons, my favorite is Frankie Valli.

I forget the names of the other three guys, but seasonally speaking, winter comes behind spring, summer, fall, parsley, sage, rosemary, and thyme.

(Thank you, Simon and Garfunkel.)

Winter is the worst season not because of sleet, which God obviously created when He had a sinus infection, or even the windchill factor, which sadistic meteorologists devised to make us feel even more miserable.

No, winter leaves me cold because, simply, it's too complicated.

Take gloves and car keys. You should because if you don't take gloves, your fingers will freeze, making it impossible to hold your car keys. And if you don't take them, the rest of you will freeze because you won't be able to get into your car and will have to trudge through a sheet of sleet (see above) that is whipping horizontally into your nostrils and will soon turn you, gloves or no gloves, into a human Popsicle.

The question is: Where do you put this stuff?

Here's where it is complicated. You might put your car keys in the front pocket of your pants (it's a good idea to wear them, too), but then you'd have to lift up the bottom of your parka (ditto) to fish the keys out of your pocket, which you can't do unless you first take off your gloves.

This, I am sure, is why keyless cars were invented, probably during the winter in a place where sleet is common.

Then there is your wallet, which you will have to fish out of your back pocket — after again taking off your gloves and lifting up the bottom of your parka — to pay by credit card or, naturally, cold cash to put gas in your car so you can drive to work.

So you figure you will outfox winter by putting everything — car keys, wallet, cellphone, gloves, ski hat, scarf, employee ID card, lip balm, hand moisturizer, flask of brandy — in the pockets of your parka so you won't have to lift it up to fish out any of those items from your pants.

Or you'll buy a tote bag in which to put all that stuff.

The problem is that if you go to the cafeteria, you'll remember that your wallet is at your desk, in either your parka or your tote bag, and not in the back pocket of your pants, where it should be.

Then there's footwear, which might normally consist of dress shoes or, if you're casual, a pair of sneakers. In winter, you have to wear boots and carry a shopping bag in which to put your shoes or sneakers so you can change into them when you get to the office. When the workday is over, you have to put your boots back on and head out to the car, where it dawns on you that you left your tote bag under your desk.

One possible solution is to bring a suitcase to work so you can stuff it with everything, including summer clothes because the heat in the office is likely to be cranked up so high that it feels like a sauna.

Speaking of which, it is not a good idea to wear only a towel unless you want to be escorted out of the building and into the arctic air, where you will, without gloves, pants, and parka, freeze to death.

So until spring springs, weather winter as best you can. And don't forget that flask of brandy.

"Out on a Limb"

Because I have acrophobia, which means I am afraid of being any higher off the ground than the top of my head, I could never imagine being a tree trimmer.

It's a condition I share with Ralph Serrano, who owns a tree company but is, unlike his brave and acrobatic employees, afraid of heights.

Even though I was standing on terra firma, which is Latin for "the ground you will land on, and then be buried under, if you fall out of a tree," I was dizzy just watching one of the crew members from Aspen Tree Service, who came over to trim some dead branches from a couple of big oaks in my backyard.

The man on the flying trapeze was Lucio, a sinewy and fearless nineteen-year-old who attached a pair of spikes to his boots and breezed up the larger of the trees until he reached a height that would give a squirrel vertigo.

As I jerked my head to look up, which made me not only a jerk but a pain in my own neck, Lucio waved for me to get out of the way. And no wonder: I was standing directly beneath a branch so massive that if it crashed onto my dense skull, I would have had a year's worth of firewood, the result being that the house would have burned to the ground because, unfortunately, I don't have a fireplace.

After I had backed safely away, Lucio revved up his chainsaw and started cutting the branch. Sawdust rained from the sky, covering my noggin and giving me a bad case of woody dandruff.

A minute later, the branch fell, its descent slowed to a gentle thud by a rope that was attached and handled by one of the other four crew members.

Lucio, a rope around him, too, swung to another branch and then to the adjacent oak, felling more lifeless limbs before gliding back down, a smile on his face and nary a drop of sweat on his brow.

I fainted.

"He's good," said Miguel, the foreman of the crew, which cut up the downed limbs.

"Aren't you afraid to be up so high?" I asked Lucio.

He shook his head and said, "I like it."

When I met Ralph, I told him that his workers were fantastic.

"They're braver than I am," he said. "The first time I saw them go up, I said, 'You guys are nuts.' You couldn't pay me to do that."

Ralph, who worked for another tree company before founding Aspen twenty years ago, recalled the first time he did a pruning job.

"I started to climb," he said. "It took me about an hour. The homeowner was staring at me. 'What are you trying to do?' he asked. I couldn't even get up the tree. I had to come back with a regular climber. I was petrified. Now I leave it to my guys to do the job."

"If tree climbing were an Olympic sport, Lucio would win a gold medal," I said.

"It's definitely a circus act," said Ralph, who's fifty-seven.

"And the height of your profession," I noted.

Ralph nodded and said, "We have plenty of puns. When people ask how business is, I'll say, 'We're branching out.' And we always go out on a limb for our customers."

"You don't," I reminded him.

"Not literally," Ralph said. "But I make sure to give them good service."

"So you're not a bump on a log," I said.

"No," he replied. "But we do haul logs away. And we offer free wood chips."

"Is that your stump speech?" I asked.

"Now it is," Ralph said.

I thanked him for a great job and told him to give Lucio and the other guys a raise.

"When it comes to tree trimming," I said, "they're a cut above."

"Bonjour, French Doors"

According to an old saying, which I just made up, when one door closes, your finger will get caught in it.

That's what happened to me, which is why I became unhinged. The door didn't, but it did lose its weatherstripping, so Sue and I went to a home improvement store to buy not one but two (because they come in pairs) French doors.

The old doors, which led from the family room to the backyard patio, wore out because they were constantly being opened and closed for ourselves and other family members, including Maggie, a canine alarm system that went off loud and clear when Kevin Morales and Matt Feeley, of A-Plus Quality Designs, came over to hang the new doors.

"I was always afraid to get French doors," I said.

"Why?" Kevin asked.

"Because," I admitted, "I don't speak French."

"So you don't know how they work?" he wondered.

"I found out when we got the old doors," I said. "Maggie knows, too. She stands there and understands what I'm saying when I ask if she has to go oui oui."

"And she's not even a French poodle," Kevin noted.

As Maggie, an American mutt, continued barking (in English), Kevin said that his stepmother is French and frequently goes back to visit her family in Paris.

"Our son-in-law Guillaume is from France," I said. "Sue and I went over when he and our daughter Lauren got married. It was wonderful."

"My stepmom's aunt still lives there," said Kevin. "She's eighty-five, but she looks like she's sixty-five."

"What's her secret?" I asked.

"She drinks wine and smokes cigarettes," he said. "And she has an apartment on the French Riviera. They live forever over there."

"Do they have French doors in France?" I inquired.

"I don't know," Kevin said. "I've never been there."

(I later asked Guillaume the same question, to which he replied, "In France, they're just called doors.")

As Kevin and Matt got themselves into a jamb, and then out of it, they unlocked some of their secrets.

"One time," Matt recalled, "we were in a cat house."

"Really?" I spluttered.

"Yeah," Matt said. "There were hundreds of cats. The place was a total mess."

"Then," Kevin chimed in, "we had a job at a mother-daughter home. In one of the rooms, they had a stripper pole. They said it was only for exercise. Meanwhile, there was a couch in there, too. You had to wonder what went on."

"Maybe," I suggested, "that was the real cathouse."

Matt, twenty-two, who studied masonry and carpentry at Alfred State College in Alfred, New York, stood outside and used a table saw to flawlessly cut strips of wood for the door frame.

"If I tried that," I told him, "my nickname would be Lefty."

"Some of my teachers were missing fingertips," Matt said. "They were really good, and I learned a lot from them, but they had been doing that kind of work for thirty years. In all that time, accidents are bound to happen."

Kevin, forty-two, who used to build modular homes and worked on the pier at South Street Seaport in New York City, said he learned his trade from his grandfather.

"He had hands of gold," said Kevin, adding that his father isn't handy at all. "It skipped a generation," he said. "In fact, nobody else in my family is handy. When something needs to be done, I'm the guy."

He and Matt were the guys to do fantastic work on our new doors. That included adding insulation, which wasn't in our old doors.

"Wasn't it freezing in this room in the winter?" Matt asked

"Now that you mention it," I said, "it was a tad chilly."

"Now it won't be," he said.

Sue and I, who had warmed up to the pair, thanked them for a job well done.

"As our son-in-law would say," I told them, "our new French doors are magnifique."

10

"Family Ties"

"Remembrance of a cool Guy"

The first time I met Carmine Pikero, the man who would become my father-in-law, he was standing in the parking lot at Stamford (now Trinity) Catholic High School. It was 1971 and he was there with my future mother-in-law, Jo, and the girl who would become my wife, their older daughter, Sue, whom I always had a crush on.

Sue and I had just graduated (she honorably, me miraculously). I walked up to Sue, kissed her, wished her a nice summer, and said I'd see her in the fall at Saint Michael's College in Vermont, where we both were going.

"Who the heck is that?!" her parents wanted to know.

"Oh, that's Jerry Zezima," Sue said casually. "He's going up to St. Mike's, too."

They must not have been too comfortable with that. Their trust was sorely tested shortly after we graduated from college. Sue and I, with our good friend Hank Richert, another Catholic High grad who also went to St. Mike's, met at the now-defunct Sittin' Room in Stamford for a Saturday night of conversation and conviviality. We all drove separate cars (I wasn't formally dating Sue at that point) and didn't overindulge, but we did stay until the place closed.

"I got in my car and started to drive home," Sue recalled when I spoke with her on the phone the next day. "As I was going up Long Ridge Road, I saw the headlights of this car behind me. I drove some more, but the car was still following me. I was getting scared. I turned onto Cedar Heights Road. So did the car. Then I turned onto Clay Hill and the car was still behind me. It followed me all the way home and up the driveway."

"Who was it?" I asked anxiously.

"My father," Sue said. "He was livid. He was out looking for me. He wanted to know who I had been with. I told him I was out with you and Hank."

All was (eventually) forgiven and I started dating Sue. When we were married, her parents warmly welcomed me into their family, just as my parents warmly welcomed Sue.

These memories came flooding back over the holidays, the first without my father-in-law, who died in July at the age of eighty-nine.

Dad loved the holidays, especially Christmas Eve, when he got to help my mother-in-law make the Feast of the Seven Fishes, the traditional Italian dinner. He wasn't a cook (boiling water was his limit), but he did help clean the shrimp and soak the baccala.

He especially liked angel-hair pasta with anchovies.

"The pasta is great," I used to say, "but I draw the line at fish with hair."

Dad, who I think would have eaten it for breakfast, would invariably reply, "You don't know what you're missing."

After all these years, I have finally relented. And now I think it's pretty good.

Dad also was handy. He had to be because he had approximately seventeen thousand tools in the basement. He must have had triplicates of every kind imaginable, including hammers, saws, and screwdrivers, which he liked to drink in the summer, though his cocktail of choice was a vodka and tonic.

Once, when Katie and Lauren were small, I "helped" Dad put up a swing set for them in the backyard of his house in Stamford. My main job was handing him tools. Afterward, I got each of us a beer.

"Thanks for your help," Dad said.

I smiled and replied, "It was nothing."

Another thing about my father-in-law was that he was a handsome dude. And a cool guy. He loved to dance and travel the world with my mother-in-law. In fact, they took the family on a cruise to Bermuda for their fiftieth wedding anniversary in 2000. I got to drive the ship. My father-in-law, calm and collected as ever, ordered a drink at the bar. I didn't blame him.

But mostly, he was a terrific husband, father, grandfather, great-grandfather, and, of course, father-in-law who set a good example for me. Now I am the father-in-law of Dave and Guillaume. I don't know if they think I'm cool, but they're great guys who have patiently and cheerfully put up with my stupid jokes.

So did my father-in-law, a good man who was much loved and has been much missed, especially during the holidays.

A toast, with a vodka and tonic: Cheers, Dad.

"The Mother of All Rehabbers"

Some people get all the breaks. That goes especially for my mother, Rosina, who recently fell and broke three vertebrae in her back. Fortunately, rehab professionals have her back, which is good because my mother would like to get rid of it.

It was the third time in five years she has fallen and broken something (first it was a leg, last year it was a wrist) and she has bounced back each time, though she didn't bounce each time she fell, which is why she has needed physical and occupational therapy.

I should mention that my mother is ninety-three years old and, as a legend of the fall, is in better shape, physically and mentally, than I am. She's absolutely amazing, which she demonstrated when I visited her in the Van Munching Rehabilitation Unit at Stamford Hospital.

"Look at the bright side," I told her. "You're running out of things to break."

"At least my head is still in one piece," my mother pointed out.

"So is mine," I said, "except it's empty."

My mother, being a good mother, just smiled.

In fact, she did a lot of smiling in Van Munching, which ought to be the name of the cafeteria. And she had a blast, especially with her friends Elaine and Eleanor, who also were there for therapy.

One evening, I joined my mother for an informal party in Elaine's room. If there had been a curfew, they would have, of course, broken it. By the time they called it a night, I was exhausted. I guess, at sixty-four, I'm too old to keep up with these nonagenarians.

I had a blast, too, when I met Mason, a therapy dog in training who was visiting from Indiana and has a foot fetish.

That was amply evident when the two-year-old tri-colored Pomeranian, who has a tri-colorful personality, became infatuated with my size-eleven sneakers.

"He loves feet," said his owner, Barbara, whose sister, Cathy, was a patient in the rehab unit.

"Mason," I said as I lifted my left foot and turned it over, "would you like to do some sole searching?"

Mason sniffed my foot and sneezed. Then he ran back to Barbara.

My mother didn't need a therapy dog because she had a therapy son. And I found out first hand, followed by my second hand, how tough therapy can be.

It wasn't tough for my mother, who's an old pro at things like the arm ergometer, a machine with two handles that a patient must push in a circular motion.

"You're doing great," said Colette, an occupational therapist who watched my mother breeze through the ten-minute exercise.

"May I try?" I asked when my mother was done.

"If you think you can do it," Colette said.

I grabbed the handles and started pushing. After three minutes, my arms were burning.

The conflagration continued when I tried to replicate my mother's performance with two-pound weights, which she lifted upward, outward, and sideways in reps of thirty each.

"I'll never make the Olympics," I admitted.

"No," Colette said. "But your mother might."

"She could have her own gym, Planet Rosina," I said.

"You should sign up," Colette suggested. "You have work to do."

That sentiment was echoed by Ed, a rehab tech, and Chris, a registered nurse who trained at The Villa at Stamford, another excellent rehabilitation facility.

"Your mom's fantastic," said Ed, who talked with her about Italian food, obviously the key to good nutrition.

"We'll have to get her out on the ice," said Chris, who like Ed is a hockey player. "Skating is good exercise."

My mother, a retired nurse who complimented Chris by saying he is a credit to their profession, replied, "I could be the puck."

Everyone in the rehab unit said my mother is amazing, not just because she is, injuries aside, in remarkable shape for someone her age, or even mine, but because she has such a positive attitude and keen sense of humor.

"You're fortunate to have such a great mom," Chris told me.

I nodded and said, "Just call it a lucky break."

"Here's Looking at You Grow Up, Kids"

If I have learned anything since becoming a grandfather, aside from the fact that diaper bags can be a great way to pull jokes on unsuspecting strangers, it is that time flies when you're having grandkids.

As proof of just how fast life whizzes past, Xavier will celebrate his first birthday tomorrow. Next week, Chloe will turn five. And little Lilly isn't so little anymore because she's almost a year and a half old.

This stuff happens every time you turn around. So here is a valuable grandparenting tip: Don't turn around. Not only will you hold time at bay, but you won't become disoriented and walk into a wall, which will, I know from experience, amuse your grandchildren.

I did this when Sue and I visited Xavier, whom we have seen only a handful of times because he lives almost three hundred miles away. Chloe and Lilly, on the other hand, live about twenty-five miles away and, on frequent visits to our house or when we go to theirs, never fail to be amused when I turn around and walk into a wall.

Still, the question is: Where does time go?

I believe it goes into the Federal Witness Protection Program. I also think time has frequent flier miles, so it probably goes to the Caribbean. And it doesn't even have the decency to send us postcards.

Speaking of flying, that's what Sue and I did when we visited Xavier, who is, I can proudly say, the smartest and most mature person in Washington, D.C.

We were picked up at the airport by Katie. She and Dave were going out of town on business later that day, which meant Sue and I would be babysitting Xavier overnight. We often FaceTime, but we hadn't seen him in person since the holidays.

"I hope he remembers us," Sue said.

"I hope he remembers my Three Stooges routines," I added, referring to our previous visit, when Xavier giggled uncontrollably at my Shemp imitations.

We had nothing to worry about. Xavier loved being with us. He still giggled when I did Shemp, chortled when I gobbled like a turkey while changing his diaper, and laughed even harder when I turned around and walked into a wall.

"He's gotten so big," Sue remarked.

"This is what happens to kids when you feed them," I said as I fed Xavier in his highchair (he was in it, not me, though I should have been since I acted more like a baby during our five-day visit than he did).

That was painfully obvious when, after Katie returned, she, Xavier, Sue, and I went to the Smithsonian.

Katie put Xavier in an Ergo, a baby carrier she wore with him facing forward so he could see what was going on. Sue carried the purses. I had the diaper bag.

When we got to the entrance, a museum guard welcomed Katie and said hello to Xavier, who smiled. Then she greeted Sue and inspected the purses. As I stepped up, I opened what I was carrying and said, "It's a diaper bag. At my age, it comes in handy."

The woman blanched. Then she broke into a broad grin and said, "I can see who the real child is here."

We had a great day at the museum, which Xavier loved. He even won friends and influenced people in the gift shop.

The next day, Dave got home, which made the rest of our visit even better.

As we were leaving, Sue and I kissed Xavier and wished him a happy first birthday.

"You're growing up fast," Sue told him.

I gobbled like a turkey, which made him laugh again. Then I flapped my arms and repeated the phrase that grandparents know so well: "Time flies."

"Goodbye, Maggie May"

There is nothing grander than being a grandparent, especially if your grandchildren are as grand as mine.

That is true of Chloe, Lilly, and Xavier, who run, walk, and toddle about on two legs.

It also was true of Maggie, who scampered about on four legs, balanced by a tail on one end and an eating machine on the other.

Lauren, who is Chloe and Lilly's mommy, was Maggie's mommy, too. Sue and I were Maggie's grandparents.

Now our family is a lot less fun and much quieter because Maggie, a whippet mix with a big personality and a voice to match, died recently at the age of thirteen.

The first thing Lauren did when she moved out of the house, officially making Sue and me empty nesters, was to get a dog. She chose a seven-month-old black and white bundle of energy she named Maggie May, after the Rod Stewart song, though Sue also called her Margaret, or Marge, or Margie, or Madge, or Mags, or some variation thereof.

Whatever the moniker, Maggie was Lauren's first baby.

When Lauren met Guillaume, Maggie accepted him right away, which said volumes because Maggie wasn't overly fond of guys of the human species, though I was an exception, too, because Maggie instinctively knew, don't ask me how, that her grandfather was an easy touch.

One of the reasons Lauren and Guillaume were such a great match was that, as Lauren later said, "I couldn't marry somebody my dog didn't like."

When Lauren was expecting Chloe, we all worried how Maggie would accept the baby. She could be territorial and jealous, but she was nothing but loving and protective when Chloe arrived. They were pals from the start, a big sister who barked and a little sister who giggled. It was play time all the time.

Due to complicated circumstances involving a house rental, Maggie lived with Sue and me the past two years, though she often saw Lauren, Chloe, Lilly, and Guillaume and loved every minute of being with all of us. She especially loved Lauren and knew she was, after all, still her mommy's dog.

And she loved Sue and the girls, who loved her right back.

It may be true that every dog has its day, but not a day went by that I didn't think there was no dog with a bigger appetite for life, as well as food of all kinds, than Maggie.

Joey Chestnut, the human vacuum cleaner who sucks down scores of wieners each year in the Nathan's Hot Dog Eating Contest, eats like a bird compared to Maggie.

We could have fed Maggie an ox and she would have wolfed it down in about two minutes. But if Sue and I sat down to dinner immediately thereafter, Maggie would stand at the table, still hungry and begging for more.

She ate so much that I feared she would explode like a canine Hindenburg, prompting me to exclaim, "Oh, the animality!"

Nonetheless, she was fussy. She would eat dry dog food only if every other source of nourishment on the planet shriveled up. She liked the treats and hearty meals that Sue gave to her on what seemed like an hourly basis. But Maggie, who was plump but not fat, sometimes got tired of one thing, which forced Sue to switch to something else. I thought Maggie should have gone to the supermarket with Sue so she could pick out what she wanted to eat that week.

Naturally, Sue would have to buy the groceries because Maggie didn't have a paying job. But she did earn her keep by being our auxiliary alarm system. That's because Maggie liked to bark. And she did, often relentlessly, if someone came to the door, or a repairman entered the house, or a squirrel scampered by, or a leaf blew past the window.

It made me wonder why dogs never get laryngitis.

But Sue and I felt secure with Maggie around.

As she got older, she had her physical challenges. We are indebted to the good folks at Jefferson Animal Hospital for taking such wonderful care of her.

The end came suddenly. Now there is a void in our house and in our hearts.

Rest well, good girl. Eat well, too. In doggy heaven, you'll never go hungry.

"A Visit From the Tooth Fairy"

For grown-ups, making money can be like pulling teeth. Kids have it so much better because they don't have to pay to have a tooth extracted. They can just wait for it to fall out. Then they can go to sleep and count on the Tooth Fairy to leave them money, which not only saves them the trouble of going to work and actually earning it, but eliminates service fees because the moola can go straight into their piggy banks.

This was the valuable dental and financial lesson learned by Chloe, who is five and a half and, thanks to the Tooth Fairy, has more shiny coins than I do because, unfortunately, I don't have a piggy bank.

Chloe lost her first tooth, the lower right central incisor, which wiggled and wobbled for a couple of weeks before succumbing to gravity and some gentle prodding by Lauren, who had prepared for the big event by looking up modern Tooth Fairy protocol.

But first, there was an announcement.

"Poppie!" Chloe chirped over the phone. "I have a loose tooth!"

"That's wonderful, Honey!" I exclaimed. "And when it falls out, you'll get a visit from the Tooth Fairy!"

"That's right, Poppie!" Chloe replied excitedly. "And she'll leave me money!"

"That's right, Chloe!" I said, continuing a conversation punctuated by exclamation points.

"I can't wait!" said Chloe, who nonetheless did not get an immediate windfall because the tooth stubbornly hung on.

It didn't fall out during a visit to the dentist. According to Lauren, Chloe announced in the office that she wouldn't be getting her adult teeth until she's forty-four.

"She also said she wasn't going to chew bubble gum until she's sixteen," Lauren reported.

The next chance for the tooth to fall out was that weekend, when Chloe spent a night with me and Sue.

"Maybe the Tooth Fairy will visit you tonight," I told Chloe.

"I hope so, Poppie," said Chloe, who opened wide to show Sue and me her delicate denticle. "Then she could visit me at my house, too."

I could see that Chloe, who is good with numbers, was already counting on doubling her money.

To facilitate a payday, I took her to Dunkin' Donuts, where she bit into a strawberry frosted doughnut with rainbow sprinkles. Unfortunately, it was too soft to knock out the tooth. So was a pizza dinner and the next morning's sausage-and-egg breakfast.

When I brought her home that afternoon, she watched a "Muppet Babies" episode devoted to the Tooth Fairy.

The video inspiration worked like a charm because that evening, Chloe's tooth finally fell out. The next day, she called to report the good news.

"I thought it was going to hurt, but it wasn't so bad," she told me.

"Did the Tooth Fairy come?" I asked.

"Yes!" Chloe replied. "She left me eight shiny coins under my pillow."

Those coins, Lauren said when she got on the phone, were quarters, so Chloe got to deposit two dollars in her piggy bank.

"She also got a certificate from the Tooth Fairy," said Lauren, who went online to print it out.

"The Tooth Fairy has a website?" I asked.

"Dad," Lauren said, "you can find anything on the internet." She added that Chloe was impressed. "She said, 'Ooh, a certificate!' It had her name on it, so it was official."

My orthodontist was impressed, too.

"Did your granddaughter get fifty cents?" Dr. Ammar Alsamawi asked during my visit to the Stony Brook University School of Dental Medicine, where, he said, the Tooth Fairy has an office.

"Even better," I told him. "She got two bucks."

"I guess the Tooth Fairy has to keep up with inflation," Dr. Alsamawi said. "I wish I'd lose my teeth so I could make money."

"First," I said, "you have to buy a piggy bank."

Chloe's is about to get fuller because when Sue and I saw her a few days later, she opened wide to show us the gap in her teeth. Then she pointed to the adjacent tooth and said, "It's getting wobbly. The Tooth Fairy is going to come back."

"Until Chloe loses the rest of her baby teeth," I told Lauren, "you'll have to keep putting your money where her mouth is."

"Cute Cousin Combo"

When two of your three grandchildren are siblings and the third one is not, that makes all of them cousins, even though the first two are not cousins of each other but only of the third, who is a cousin of the first two but not of himself.

That makes the cuckoo who concocted this cockamamie cousin conundrum a grandfather twice removed, which means he should have been removed from a family get-together twice already but, to the consternation of everyone else, keeps coming back.

It happened when Sue and I were visited by Chloe, who is five and a half; her little sister, Lilly, who is almost two; and their cousin, Xavier, who's a year and a half.

We are fortunate to see Chloe and Lilly frequently because they live about twenty-five miles away, but it's not often that we see Xavier because he lives almost three hundred miles away. So when there is a chance for all of them to get together, we jump at the opportunity, Sue gracefully with a perfect landing, me clumsily with a stubbed toe and a score that would have gotten me thrown out of the Olympics.

And it takes an Olympian effort to keep up with all of them because they are full of energy, while I am full of, well, diapers, which I have never minded changing for any of them and still do for the youngest two.

Now that I have come clean about it, I should add that the kids have distinct personalities. Chloe relishes her role as big sister and big cousin and takes an almost maternal approach to Lilly and Xavier, showering them with love. Chloe also has a great sense of humor. At dinner during a visit by my mother, Rosina, known to her great-grandchildren as Gigi, Chloe told jokes.

"Knock, knock," she told the assemblage, which included my nephew Blair and my niece Whitney.

"Who's there?" we all inquired.

"Boo."

"Boo who?"

"Don't cry," Chloe responded with perfect timing. "It's just a joke."

When the line got a big laugh, she beamed. Then she told more jokes.

Lilly is the pistol of the trio. She doesn't tell jokes, but she gets laughs anyway.

"Nini! Poppie! Nini! Poppie!" she chatters to Sue and me. She'll go up to our Amazon Echo and shout, "Alexa!" When the device activates, Lilly says, "Moana! Moon!" Then she'll break into a spontaneous dance when a song from the soundtrack to one of her favorite movies, such as "Moana" or "Sing," starts playing.

Lilly also eats more than Chloe and Xavier combined but is still a peanut who's about five pounds lighter than Xavier, even though she's five months older than he is.

Xavier is a sweet, quiet boy with a perennial smile and an infectious giggle, which I love to trigger with silly sounds and funny faces, which I ordinarily make anyway. Unlike Chloe and Lilly, who love Sue but are more attached to me, Xavier loves me but is more attached to Sue, who exulted at finally being the favorite grandparent by hoisting him into her arms, no easy feat since he's a big boy, and doing a victory lap around the family room.

Xavier also loves Chloe and called for her after she went home. When she and Lilly returned a couple of days later, Xavier hugged Chloe. He and Lilly are more competitive, vying for the same toys, but they get along well, too.

That was evident when the three of them romped in the backyard, splashing in the kiddie pool, running under the sprinkler, and drawing on the patio with chalk.

Chloe drew hopscotch squares, then counted in French as she hopped.

"I love doing hopscotch in French!" she exclaimed.

"Magnifique, Chloe!" I said.

"Merci, Poppie!" she replied.

Lilly and Xavier added their artistry, not only to the patio but to our outdoor furniture. The Louvre would have loved it.

But not as much as Sue and I love our grandchildren. It was great to have them together, which doesn't happen too often. We can't wait for the next time.

Till then, I'll keep trying to figure out that cockamamie cousin conundrum. Maybe when all the kids come back, they can explain it to me.

"Isn't It Romantic?"

When you've been married for forty years, as Sue and I have been, you want to celebrate your anniversary in a big way, by doing something wonderful and memorable during a week of fun and frolic, all while expressing your eternal devotion to your beloved spouse.

So I got my teeth cleaned and Sue had a root canal.

These were only two of the many romantic ways we marked this landmark event, which was so action-packed that we needed five full days to cram it all in.

It should be noted that we spent this time at home, not in some tropical resort with postcards, palm trees, and swim-up bars, which only would have distracted us from doing such exciting things as shoveling snow and babysitting our granddaughters.

That's exactly what we did on our anniversary, when Mother Nature spared no expense in gifting us with a spring storm that dumped six inches of snow on our driveway.

Instead of wearing a bathing suit and flip-flops, with a margarita in hand, I donned a parka and boots, with a shovel in hand, and headed out into the arctic air.

"Have fun!" Sue said as she blew me a kiss.

When I came back in, cold and tired, I found a waterfall — not like in Hawaii, where Sue and I honeymooned — that was cascading through the ceiling from an upstairs bathroom, where Guillaume had just taken a shower.

"Shall we call a plumber to help us celebrate our anniversary?" I asked Sue.

She declined when the leak stopped and said that she and Lauren were going shopping. Since Guillaume was going to work, I would be in charge of babysitting Chloe and Lilly. It was the most fun I had all day.

Later, after everyone left and Sue and I were alone, we had a romantic candlelight dinner featuring leftovers.

"It doesn't get any better than this," I said as Sue and I toasted each other with boxed wine.

"Happy anniversary, dear," she replied sweetly.

The next day, which was Tuesday, I proved that I would do anything for my wife short of painting the hallway by driving her to the orthodontist's office so she could have a root canal.

"Don't worry," I said reassuringly. "It won't hurt."

"That's easy for you to say," Sue replied nervously.

"I know," I told her. "That's why I said it."

As it turned out, I was right: It didn't hurt at all. It didn't hurt Sue, either. But it did knock her out, which is why she spent the afternoon napping while I made myself useful by having cocktails.

On Wednesday, I had an appointment with my dermatologist, who will turn forty later this year.

"I've been married as long as you've been alive," I said.

"I've been married for twelve years," he responded, "but it feels like forty."

By the afternoon, Sue was feeling much better, so we spent the rest of the day at the outlets, shopping for sneakers, shoes, and, most important, a new pair of boots.

"In case," I explained to Sue, "it snows again."

On Thursday, the action continued when I got a haircut. After I told my barber, Maria, about my anniversary week, she said, "You'll need another week to recover."

That afternoon, Sue and I went to a travel agency to see if we could book a vacation to a warmer locale later in the year.

Lindsay, our travel consultant, said, "You're having a busy week. You need to get away."

Friday morning, I got my teeth cleaned. After I told Margaret, the hygienist, all about the exciting things Sue and I had done to celebrate our anniversary, she said, "All that's missing is a colonoscopy."

That night, Sue and I went out to dinner at a nice Italian restaurant called Grana, where we were serenaded by Brett Chizever, a bartender who also has theater experience and once played Rooster Hannigan in a road version of "Annie."

In a beautiful operatic voice, Brett, thirty, sang us a Gershwin tune called "Love Is Here to Stay."

His rendition earned a round of applause.

"Happy fortieth anniversary, you two lovebirds," Brett said.

"Thank you," Sue replied with a wide smile.

"Believe me," I added, "this is the most romantic thing that's happened to us all week."

EPILOGUE

"There are no secrets in our family," Sue has often said. "Our lives are an open book."

Actually, this is the fourth book in which I have written about our family. Since you have opened it, you know Sue is right.

As a humor columnist, I am always looking for things to write about. More often than not, I don't have to look far, which is good because my eyes aren't what they used to be. In fact, they used to be martini olives. Those were the days!

At any rate, most of those things happen in my own home. And they involve, the vast majority of the time, my family.

That's why you know so much about us. But you may have seen yourself and your family in this book, too. Whether you are a grandparent, an empty nester, a baby boomer, or all of the above, you have undoubtedly done the same things I have. You just haven't written about them. And I would advise you not to because I need the money.

Even your kids — especially if they have kids who happen to be your grandchildren — can see themselves. They're probably laughing and saying, "Good old Dad! He's such a dolt, but we love him anyway. By the way, Mom, can you guys babysit for us next weekend?"

And you nod and smile and devise even more ways to spoil and corrupt your grandchildren. If your kids don't like it, tough. Then you and your spouse can go to a vineyard and have a good time by yourselves.

The question now is: What's next?

The answer: Another glass of wine.

But you also want a more permanent answer: Retirement.

Maybe you're already there. Sue and I aren't, but we are hoping it happens soon. Then we'd have even more time to spend with Chloe, who is five and a half; Lilly, who just turned two; and Xavier, who's a year and a half. We'd also be able to enjoy one of life's great luxuries: climbing into bed at night and not turning on the alarm. Whenever you wake up, it's OK. What a concept!

Of course, we'd miss being stuck in rush-hour traffic every weekday, both to and from work, while our engines and our brains overheated, but I am sure we'd get over it.

Best of all, we'd have more excellent adventures. I may even get another open book out of it.